The First 100 Feet

The First 100 Feet

Options for Internet and Broadband Access

edited by Deborah Hurley and James H. Keller

A Publication of the Harvard Information Infrastructure Project

The MIT Press, Cambridge, Massachusetts, and London, England

This book was printed and bound in the United States of America.

Library of Congress Cataloging-in-Publication Data

The first 100 feet: options for Internet and Broadband access /
edited by Deborah Hurley and James H. Keller.
    p.   cm.—(Publication of the Harvard Information
Infrastructure Project)
    Includes bibliographical references and index.
    ISBN 0-262-58160-4 (pbk. : alk. paper)
    1. Telecommunication lines—United States. 2. Broadband
communication systems. 3. Internet (Computer network) 4. Electric
utilities—United States. 5. Infrastructure (Economics)—United
States. I. Hurley, Deborah. II. Keller, James H. III. Series.
TK5103.15.F57   1999
384.3'2—dc21   99-25725
                                                          CIP

Contents

Foreword

Lewis M. Branscomb

The telephone industry grew through the massive corporate investment of regulated revenues into a circuit-switched network of ever greater reach and capacity. The ability of anyone with a telephone to call anyone else similarly equipped was the "killer application" that grew in value as a result of network externalities. In contrast, the Internet's growth has been made possible by the free market decision of thousands of firms and millions of households to invest in general-purpose computer equipment. A dozen or so application types convinced people that an investment that was typically well over $1,000 was worth it. With the addition of an inexpensive modem, this allowed Internet architects to leverage the computing power in the users' own equipment to create the intelligence needed for a universally interoperable computer network. The rest, as they say, is history.

Will end users be equally willing to invest in capital equipment in the $500 to $1,000 range to empower a new range of Internet capabilities that require more bandwidth than the telephone line quality and modem can support? If so, what mechanism for matching the internal bandwidth of their computers to the capacity of the digital communications infrastructure will consumers select? There are many possibilities, from cable TV to hard-wired telephone lines, to wireless and satellite communications, and even to the electric power line infrastructure. If not, how can we expect broadband capability to diffuse throughout the U.S. infrastructure, given that, generally speaking, early adopters of broadband are not geographically concentrated? Thus it is not reasonable to expect the facilities-based communications firms to pay for connecting all their customers to broadband service all at once. The PC solved that problem initially by its property as a standalone device. The failure of your neighbor to buy a PC did not decrease your own satisfaction (or aggravation) with your PC investment.

Thus the options and incentives for consumers to invest in the first 100 feet from their homes to the nearest communications channel in the street will be critical to the empowerment of multimedia and other high-bandwidth applications. This book explores this set of choices and their likely efficacy.

The workshop in which these issues were debated was a cooperative venture of four organizations: the Harvard Information Infrastructure Program (HIIP) in the university's John F. Kennedy School of Government shared the sponsorship with the Freedom Forum (which hosted the meeting in their beautiful facility), the National Economic Council (whose staff have played leading roles in the development of broadband infrastructure), and the U.S. Department of Energy, which provided much of the funding for the workshop and for this book, and brought into the discussion the possible role of electric utilities as a potential broadband interconnection channel.

We are grateful to the members of the project steering committee for the vision and direction they provided this activity: Robert Aiken and John Cavallini of the U.S. Department of Energy; Brian Kahin, founding director of the Harvard Information Infrastructure Project (HIIP) and now Senior Policy Advisor for Information Infrastructure at the White House Office of Science and Technology Policy; Tom Kalil of the National Economic Council; James Keller, formerly HIIP Associate Director; Adam Powell of the Freedom Forum; Mary Anne Scott, U.S. Department of Energy; and Steven Rivkin, Attorney.

Additional support for this and other work of the Harvard Information Infrastructure Project is provided by Advanced Network and Services, the Ameritech Foundation, AT&T, Bellcore, the Defense Advanced Research Projects Agency, EDS, Hughes Electronics, IBM, the IBM International Foundation, Motorola, the National Science Foundation, NYNEX, Time Warner Cable, and the W. K. Kellogg Foundation.

We are especially indebted to Nora O'Neil, our Project Coordinator, for keeping this project on track, to Miriam Avins and Mary Albon for their fine work as copy editors, and to Deborah Hurley and James Keller as editors of this volume. Andrew Russell, Ajay Kuntamukala, Dean Berlin, and Stephen Feinson also played critical roles in the preparation of this manuscript. Lastly, this work draws on a broad community of scholars, policymakers, and members of the business community, and we are grateful for their efforts in advancing understanding of the issues and opportunities related to connecting the first 100 feet.

Introduction

Deborah Hurley and James Keller

In many respects, the vision of a rapidly expanding, highly functional and content-rich Internet appears to be coalescing. The
Internet continues to grow at an astounding rate. Internet domains
continue to double each year, and the capacity of Internet backbone networks is rapidly increasing. This growth is real and will
continue, but it alone will not be enough to bring about the
transformative change that has been ascribed to the Internet.
Investment in Internet connectivity has been at the core of the
network. This investment has been enhanced by large institutions
connecting many users to the network through a common pipe.
Extending this investment to enable high-speed network access
from individual homes and small businesses has been much a more
difficult process. The potential cost has been estimated in the
billions of dollars. As a result, ubiquitous high-speed access has
been slow in coming, and the associated benefits of a truly networked
society remain in the future.

In contrast to traditional telecommunications, the history of the
Internet can be described as a case of bottom-up infrastructure
investment. Internet technology allows end-users to make their
own investments in intelligent infrastructure, thereby increasing
their capability to access the rest of the world. The vast majority of
Internet investment is user investment in computers and local
networking equipment. The incremental cost that an institution
typically pays to connect to the Internet is tiny compared to the
investment made in these local resources. The cost of Internet

connectivity to a large institution is typically on the order of $10–15 per user per year. The amortized cost of local computing and communications resources is in excess of $1,000 per person per year. Extending the bottom-up model to residential and small business users offers an opportunity to explore local access alternatives beyond the traditional model of large centralized investment.

This book looks at options for Internet and broadband access from the perspective of home owners, apartment complexes, and small businesses. It will evaluate opportunities and obstacles for "bottom-up" infrastructure development and the implications for traditional and alternative providers at the neighborhood, regional, and national levels. This approach is considered in recognition of the huge cost barriers to top-down investment, and as a means of giving smaller users greater power in the marketplace.

The book is intended to challenge business and policymakers to rethink fundamental issues in telecommunications policy by recasting the "problem of the last 100 feet" as "opportunities for the first 100 feet." This paradigm shift suggests consumer/property owner investment as an answer to the dilemma of whether there should be one or two wires into the home. The book will survey alternative options for local connection to the Internet from the perspective of homeowners, apartment owners, small businesses, and others with an interest in investing in end-user equipment and real estate. It will consider prospects for broadly distributed infrastructure investment and potential roles for utility companies, special assessment districts, municipalities, PCS providers, CAPs, IXCs, and Internet access providers, as well as telcos and cable companies. It will consider strategies and policies for local interconnection and interoperability among LECs, alternative carriers, and Internet access providers.

The book will investigate constraints on and incentives for user infrastructure investment at federal, state, and local levels; whether and how trenching, conduit, and rights-of-way should be unbundled to promote consumer/property owner investment and competition among heterogeneous providers; and the need for and feasibility of interconnection at third-party or publicly maintained neighborhood access points. It will look at synergy with other policy goals and economic interests, such as energy demand management. Finally, in assessing user investment as a driver for two-way broadband, it asks how scenarios for Internet access will affect broadband scenarios by stimulating demand for high-bandwidth connectivity.

Rationale

The growth of the Internet has been propelled in significant part by user investments in infrastructure: computers, internal wiring, and the connection (dial-up line, leased line, microwave link) to the Internet service provider. This "bottom-up" investment minimizes the investment burden facing service providers, since customers share the cost of the infrastructure and providers have no obligation to develop the infrastructure out to all potential users. Barriers to entry for service providers are low, and users retain flexibility in choosing among providers.

The rapidly growing mass of Internet users, applications, and resources is now shaping demand for underlying infrastructure, so that plans for new infrastructure are driven increasingly by data rather than voice and video. There are opportunities to attract new customers instead of competing head-on for old ones. Unlike voice and video, there are incremental upgrade paths for data users and demand for upgraded access is readily stimulated by experience. Higher-bandwidth connections are desired by a wide spectrum of users, from those who work at home to recreational users of the World Wide Web.

The value of continuous, rather than dial-up, connection to the Internet is less widely appreciated because it is a qualitative improvement. Continuous connectivity (which can be provided by unswitched technologies, such as spread-spectrum wireless and cable modems) obviates tying up a telephone line, enables instant delivery of email and other time-sensitive information, and allows small businesses to advertise and publish directly to the net. Most importantly, it can enable real-time energy management, with attendant cost savings, that may support major infrastructure investment, which the advent of residential "wheeling" may induce consumers to make on their own. A personal computer or an inexpensive router might serve as a gateway extending Internet functions to other computers in the home to manage utility demand, operate security systems, and control lights, sound equipment, and other household appliances.

As telecommunications and electric utilities are deregulated, investment decisions will devolve into the hands of consumers, where they may be made with greater knowledge of particular benefits and tradeoffs. At the same time, new technologies, such as wireless and data transmission over power lines, will increase consumer options. There may be a variety of options for configuring "the last mile," with different balances between user-provided and centrally provided facilities. Homeowners and small businesses may have opportunities to connect to different suppliers at the curb, on the roof, on the side of the house, or somewhere in between.

The early government role and subsequent commercial practices have facilitated interconnection of Internet service providers, but the limited choices at the local level—the "last mile" as well as the "last 100 feet"—may make interconnection an issue. At present, many local Internet access providers do not interconnect directly, and traffic is sometimes routed to one of the few national exchange points hundreds of miles away. Opportunities for interconnection, along with policies on access, may determine whether intermediary transport providers, such as utility companies, emerge to link homeowner facilities at the curb with high-bandwidth Internet service providers.

This analysis of "the first hundred feet" recognizes that need and demand will naturally vary greatly from home to home and from neighborhood to neighborhood. Much depends on whether there are business or telecommuting needs that may be met by individual investments in upgraded access. While this analysis looks to the Internet, it raises the issue of how the bottom-up model will affect the traditional model of a centrally provided universal service. Given basic technology that is nonproprietary and virtually commoditized, some argue that Internet service is becoming the common denominator platform on which all other services can be carried. The absence of service class priority has hampered use of real-time voice and video on the Internet, but this will soon change with the implementation of protocols that allow bandwidth reservation and packet-level service priority (RSVP and IPv6).

Overview

The first section of this book explores market issues associated with bottom-up infrastructure development and market demand. David Gabel and Milton Mueller start by describing issues related to user investment in infrastructure development. This chapter takes a historical perspective, describing the development of rural telephony at the turn of the century. A key difference between this system and today's Internet is the reliance on centralized network intelligence—often in the form of an operator switching calls by hand. On the Internet, connectivity may be managed from intelligent endpoints, allowing users to invest independently without the transaction costs of coordination, but requiring greater technological sophistication to configure CPE and to interact with various access media.

In the next chapter, Branko Gerovac and Dave Carver present a set of criteria for evaluating infrastructure development options. This includes traditional factors related to technology architecture as well as business and policy criteria. These criteria are applied to a series of deployment scenarios, ranging from top-down fiber-to-the-home investment to a scalable, peer-to-peer microcellular model. The last chapter in this section, by John Carey, describes adoption patterns for new technology, as additional background for understanding issues in the deployment of new types of Internet access. Carey explores the price patterns and penetration rates for each of the major innovations in information and communications. He presents a set of lessons drawn from these other technology areas to evaluate the potential for adoption of new access technologies.

The second section of the book looks at a variety of models for bottom-up investment in the first 100 feet. In each case, these are models that look beyond the traditional telecommunications network infrastructure to leverage new technical opportunities. Solutions explored include spread spectrum wireless, satellite, and the use of electric power networks.

Dave Hughes leads off this section by describing license-free spread-spectrum radio frequency as a low-cost, scalable access solution. The spread-spectrum model is very much counter to the traditional telecommunications services model, where, as in the case of cellular telephony, the equipment is given away and network access is sold at a premium. With spread spectrum, wireless radio receiver/transmitters are sold and the spectrum is free, perhaps the ultimate in bottom-up investment. Radios are currently in the $2,000+ range, but sub-$500 radios are now in development. Even at the higher rate, the radio costs less than several months of comparable speed access. In the next chapter David Beyer, Mark Vestrich, and J.J. Garcia-Luna-Aceves take the spread-spectrum model a step further, describing how it may be deployed to create rooftop community networks that facilitate Internet connectivity throughout a neighborhood. This model brings the same type of scale economies that have benefitted universities and large organizations to networks of homes and small businesses.

Michael Propp then explores the use of electric power lines for data communications. Propp describes how a communications signal can be modulated over existing power line infrastructure, including existing applications in Europe and opportunities for future deployment. Markets already exist for communications applications, such as energy demand management, which may help justify the investment required to upgrade the grid for data communications.

Bryan Vu focuses on satellite broadband possibilities. He examines the various satellite proposals and evaluates them relative to one another and to existing terrestrial services. He also describes the regulatory hurdles that these systems will face.

The final section of the book describes the opportunities and challenges faced by two nontraditional providers—cities and utilities—in becoming providers of telecommunications services. This includes the institutional and regulatory hurdles that local communities and electric utilities will face in providing solutions to the challenge of the first 100 feet. The section begins with a chapter by Andrea Johnson describing the role of cities as developers, regulators, and users of telecommunications networks. These networks may support city functions, promote economic development, and expand universal access. The chapter pays particular attention to the implications for cities of the Telecommunications Act of 1996.

Steven Rivkin builds upon Propp's description of the ability to modulate a communications signal over a power line and explores the role for electric utilities as providers of communications services. Rivkin describes the shared histories of the communications and electric power industries and the implications of current regulatory change and market development in each industry. He concludes that power companies are well positioned to play an important role as providers of communications services. This story is continued by Bernice McIntyre, who provides more detailed background on the changing regulatory environment and the regulatory challenges utilities may face in becoming communications services providers. This chapter provides an overview of initiatives now underway by both public and private utilities to provide communications services and delineates the factors that must be considered to ensure fair competition among industries governed by different laws and regulations.

The final chapter of the book, by Lon Berquist and August Grant, looks in depth at the experience of cities in developing advanced information infrastructures for the benefit of their citizens. The chapter uses the city of Austin, Texas, as a case study and, combining this example with the experiences of several other municipalities that have been early movers, presents a set of lessons for the development of municipal infrastructure.

Market Issues for the First 100 Feet

Household Financing of the First 100 Feet?

David Gabel and Milton Mueller

Currently, most households obtain access to the Internet through dial-up modems. Although modem technology has improved dramatically in the 1990s, there is a widespread belief that users must adopt fundamentally different technology in order to exploit the full potential of the Internet and, particularly, new video and graphics-oriented services. New high-speed data access technologies are likely to come from one of four suppliers: telephone companies, electric power networks, cable networks, or satellite systems.[1] The first three suppliers would need to make large investments in cable and electronics. Such a course is risky because the investments are sunk; if subscribers do not use the installed technology, the equipment has almost no resale value. It is unlikely that a telephone, cable, or electric facility provider will find it economical to recover its facilities. It may be possible to recoup the electronics, such as a high-speed modem, but only with high transaction costs.

Capital outlays of this sort are risky not only due to asset specificity, but also because of the great uncertainty in gauging demand and predicting the course of various substitutes for the services. When businesses consider upgrading the distribution facilities linking residences to the public network to make higher-bandwidth data and video services possible, they usually find that the current market and industry structure scarcely justify the investment in new infrastructure. It is difficult to see how the revenue streams that can be projected for such services can recover the expenses. As a result of the unhealthy prospective returns, many businesses have scaled back their infrastructure plans announced a few years ago. For example, most telephone companies have drawn back from plans to upgrade their networks for provision of video dialtone.[2]

In order to address this problem, many nations are changing their regulation of communication businesses to improve the earnings potential of customer access investments. Barriers that separate voice, data, and video markets are being removed in order to enhance the feasibility of facility-based competition.[3] Even with these changes in place, businesses are investing incrementally in new customer access networks. The rapid deployment of a high-speed data network to the home is unlikely.

This chapter explores the practicality of consumers investing in the infrastructure themselves. Instead of relying on third-party capital supplied by private businesses, perhaps consumer dollars might finance the construction of a new generation of high-speed links between the network and the household. The chapter first demonstrates that subscriber-financed access lines played an important role in developing the nation's telephone network. This precedent illuminates the salient factors that made investments by consumers a viable path. After examining the telephone case, the chapter addresses the practicality of pursuing a similar course today.

User Capital and the Development of Rural Telephony

During the period of 1893 to 1911, rural telephone service expanded rapidly in the United States because of competition between AT&T and independent local exchange companies. Until the Bell system's fundamental patents on its telephone equipment began to expire in 1893, the Bell system largely ignored rural America. It neither extended telephone service to those who lived in rural areas, nor allowed independent companies that wished to offer telephone service to the countryside to buy or manufacture patented equipment. Bell followed this investment strategy because it believed that the telephone was an urban technology that would follow the developmental path of the telegraph. In fact, the

Bell companies seriously underestimated the demand for telephony in rural areas and small towns, and its refusal to allow others to develop markets in which it had little or no interest was one of the high costs of the patent-based monopoly.[4]

For a variety of reasons, investment capital was scarce during this period of American history, particularly in rural markets. The scarcity of outside capital did not deter the farmers and businessmen in rural areas. Instead of depending on regional or national markets to fund the development of local telephone companies, local independent telephone companies relied almost exclusively on local capital and labor. Subscribers in rural communities were frequently required to buy stock in the new telephone companies. The sale of stock certificates to customers, at prices ranging from $25 to $50, provided sufficient money to cover the cost of installing their telephones. These installation fees served as the primary source of capital for many companies.[5]

The developers of rural telephony also held down the financial cost of constructing a telephone company by requiring subscribers to donate labor and material. Customers were often required to build the drop-line that connected their farmhouse with the distribution line running down the main road. Rural subscribers were also asked to aid in the setting and stringing of the distribution lines and wires that connected the houses to the switchboard.[6] In this way, rural companies were able to overcome the shortage of capital that was partly responsible for the delayed development of telephony.[7]

The size, organization, and construction methods of the independents varied considerably. Sometimes rural "roadline" companies were established in which six to 12 farmers would share one line. The line would be constructed by stringing together the roadside wires that marked the farmers' property lines. When first established, the physical plant of the roadline companies did not connect into any switchboard. The customers could only contact other customers on their line.[8]

Competing, commercial telephone companies also developed in small towns and villages. The independent telephone exchanges were often established by doctors who wanted to enhance their ability to communicate with patients and other doctors. In addition, local businessmen recognized that the telephone enhanced the commercial standing of their city; after a telephone system was installed, residents in surrounding communities found it easier to transact business with village merchants.[9] The village exchanges of the Bell system and the independents competed vigorously to interconnect the roadline companies to their exchanges and long-distance lines.

The financing of the village and roadline companies differed. The village companies were more likely to be funded by a few professionals and businessmen who saw an opportunity or a need to enhance the value of their businesses by improving the infra-structure of the town. The roadline companies relied almost exclusively on subscriber contributions. Farmers were more con-cerned with the social benefits of the phone, most noticeably how it reduced their level of isolation.[10]

In larger towns and cities, independent phone companies com-peted with the Bell system to provide local exchange service and regional long-distance lines. These firms usually obtained their financing from a few local professionals and businessmen, such as lawyers and railroad executives. But in at least four competitive Wisconsin exchanges (Wausau, Merrill, Rhinelander, and Grand Rapids), the stock holding was not concentrated in the hands of any one or two groups of businessmen. The founders of the Wausau Telephone Company established a rule that prohibited anyone from holding more shares of capital stock than the number of phones rented for personal use. They did this in order to ensure that no party would establish a pricing policy that would allow the firm to earn excessive profits.[11]

In order to provide high-quality toll service, the city exchanges constructed by the commercial independent companies used the same construction practices as the Bell system. In order to maxi-mize the quality of voice transmission, the independents used metallic circuits to connect customers to the central office and for interexchange circuits. Rural exchanges, which generally used single-wire, grounded iron conductors, were sometimes refused interconnection with the independent toll network because of the larger exchange's concern about maintaining high-quality ser-vice.[12]

Competition between overlapping Bell system and independent exchanges was phased out between 1914 and 1925, in order to eliminate the subscriber fragmentation caused by the existence of separate telephone systems. Nevertheless, more than 1,000 independent telephone companies remained in operation. Most were in the rural areas that the Bell system was still not interested in serving; some metropolitan areas such as Rochester, New York and southern California were also served by larger independents. Most of the customer-operated roadline systems were eventually commercialized and taken over by either Bell or independent companies. But there are still some cooperatively owned telephone systems in rural areas today.

Would Customer-Financed Networks Succeed Today?

Would it be possible today to bring new telecommunications services to residential households through customer-financed networks? There are some strong similarities between the events at the beginning and the end of the 20th century, but the differences are important.

Demand Uncertainty

One of the biggest impediments to investments in telecommunications infrastructure is the uncertain demand for new services. Firms are reluctant to invest in infrastructure modernization because of the uncertainty regarding consumer interest in the new products that may be sold through the technology. Telecommunications suppliers, for example, hesitated to deploy high-speed telecommunications networks in Iowa, Nebraska, and North Carolina, despite the fact that the governments of these states clearly desired the deployment of leading-edge technology. The telephone companies in these states were concerned that the demand for new services would not materialize and refused to begin construction until the state governments shared the risk of the undertakings.[13] Many other suppliers have exhibited a similar hesitancy about infrastructure investments.[14]

The telephone system also faced a kind of demand uncertainty at the turn of the century. The Bell system misunderstood the nature of telephone demand, assuming that it was primarily restricted to an urban, business market. As a result, it targeted investment to cities and ignored small towns, farm areas, and short-haul toll lines. Giving end-users an opportunity to make their own investments was a huge stimulus to telephone development, largely because it allowed the real pattern of demand to emerge spontaneously. Consumer investments helped to reveal that suppliers had over-looked pockets of intense demand. Telephone demand is characterized by positive consumption externalities, which means that the value of service to one consumer is enhanced when other consumers join the network. The existence of this "network" externality meant that investments by rural customers in outlying areas increased the value of the commercial exchanges in villages and towns once they were interconnected. Thus, consumer financing also stimulated the development of long-distance markets and local-exchange markets in nearby areas.

The importance of end-user investments as part of the "discovery process" that defines and develops the market may hardly be overstated. End-user investments are more fungible and may better respond to highly variable levels of demand than investments made by large-scale, capital-intensive carriers. Whereas the latter must worry about the common denominator of demand in a neighborhood and how an investment in that neighborhood would be recovered from aggregate usage patterns, a consumer only has to worry about her own needs. And who knows those needs better than the consumer?

There is, however, an important difference between early telephony and today's market for advanced communication services. The self-financed telephone networks of the early 1900s provided services and products that were already available and accepted in other parts of the country. Farmers knew exactly what they wanted from a telephone—they knew that they could use the instrument to overcome social isolation and to expedite commercial transactions. Telephone service constituted a tangible, significant improvement in the farm dweller's quality of life. Indeed, many farmers had tried for years prior to the expiration of the Bell patents to construct their own telephones and lines, but were prevented from doing so by Bell system patent infringement lawsuits.[15]

Far from being plagued by the kind of demand uncertainty facing new and enhanced telecommunications services today, telephone companies faced a huge, pent-up demand for telephone service around the turn of the century. The value of many new services, such as video-on-demand, extensive home shopping, or video dial tone, is purely speculative and, in some cases, they differ only subtly from services currently delivered by cable television, to put it charitably. Thus, it is unrealistic to expect consumers to finance on their own initiative any part of the infrastructure needed to support advanced telecommunications services that do not yet exist. But for services like Internet access, for which the nature of the service and its perceived benefits are clear and many users consider the current infrastructure inadequate, consumers may well have the incentive to take the initiative.

Standardized Technology

Farmers not only understood the value of the telephone, but also the technology. Through their trade associations, the independent telephone companies quickly established construction standards that emulated the methods adopted by the Bell system.[16] The technology was not especially complicated. Iron or copper wire was strung from a household to a manual switchboard in the nearest town. When rural customers decided to finance their own network, the technology choices were rather limited: copper or iron wire, ground or loop return.

In contrast, an investor today must consider multiple technologies—e.g., ATM, frame-relay, fiber, hybrid fiber-coaxial, SONET, compression, fiber, multiplexer, coaxial cables, power sources, set-top boxes—and try to make a reasonable forecast of future technologies. An early adopter wants to avoid making a commitment to a technology that will not be compatible with other communications technologies or that will be expensive relative to facilities that may be deployed in the near future. Established suppliers are having a difficult time determining the elements of a sensible network architecture. Residential consumers hardly have the expertise or the resources to evaluate the comparative advantages of the different technologies.

While users face some of the same uncertainties with regard to their investments in computer terminals and software, imperfect standardization and heterogeneous choices have not prevented them from making substantial investments in PCs, modems, and other customer premises equipment (CPE). However, the degree of uncertainty and heterogeneity is much greater for access facilities than for CPE. Consumers obtain information about computers from magazines, friends, and associates at work. All these information sources are inexpensive relative to the cost of assessing the merits of different customer access technologies. Due to this high cost of information, there are few early adopters of customer access facilities. Until a substantial "critical mass" of users exists and creates an inexpensive market for information, users may find themselves committed to inferior, but well accepted, technology.[17]

Deciding upon the appropriate technology is not as difficult when the use of the network is well defined. Through the Net Day project, volunteers, in cooperation with private companies, wired schools, and libraries to provide them with Internet access. The success of the Net Day project shows that collective resources may be marshaled to provide an improved infrastructure at a low cost, once a community decides to adopt a particular platform. However, the technology used in these undertakings is hardly leading edge; the goal was to provide a 28.8 kilobyte-per-second connection over the existing telephone network.[18] As with the development of rural telephony, the Net Day project is expanding the use of an existing technology, not deploying new technology of uncertain applications and value.

The danger of installing state-of-the-art technology in anticipation of new uses is illustrated by recent developments in North Carolina. Potential users were directly involved in the planning of a statewide, educational, interactive video network. Despite many expressions of demand, the high cost of using the system has led to a slower rate of adoption by schools than expected. Some of the schools that the state anticipated would use the network only wanted to buy access to the Internet at higher speeds than were available over conventional telephone lines, which is a less expensive service to provide. Many did not want to pay for the capacity to send and receive video images. Thus, the rates that the state pays to the telephone companies are based on estimates of use that have not been met. "These rates, and ultimately the rates charged to users, may have to go up to allow the telephone companies to recover their investment, further discouraging use of the statewide network."[19]

This example illustrates some of the inherent limitations of supply-side-driven efforts to gauge demand. Companies make investments based on what users tell them they want, but until the users actually have to pay for the service for a significant period, their real utility function cannot be discerned. In a user-driven network, there is much less of a communication gap between the investment and the value. Users make specific investments (e.g., an improved modem) to achieve specific results. While they may make errors or be disappointed with the results, the risk of loss is much smaller than when such a decision is made on the scale of an entire city, state, or nation.

Outsourcing vs. In-Sourcing

If significant numbers of consumers want something new and better from their access lines, is it reasonable to expect an increasingly heterogeneous and competitive market for telecommunications channels to provide them with improved access, or must they invest in equipment themselves? If end-users want higher-speed access to the Internet, one alternative is to build it themselves. Another possibility is to hope that entrepreneurs will develop alternative access technologies, such as satellite-based Internet access, cable modems, Integrated Services Digital Networks (ISDN), or a new wireless service in the Personal Communication Service (PCS) band. Yet another alternative is consumer investment in increasingly powerful and sophisticated on-premises equipment (i.e., computers, modems, consumer electronics). Such investments may provide the data compression capabilities to expand bandwidth or may permit consumers to use radio or infrared transmission to bypass the bottleneck of the local access line. A combination of the latter two alternatives (service provision by competitors and improvements in CPE investments) is more likely to be optimal for consumers, rather than taking over the first 100 feet.

CPE equipment provides the consumer with more flexibility than investment in the first 100 feet. For example, different modems may be connected to a computer, depending on whether satellite, cable, wireless, or telephone access to the Internet is selected. Modems might even be supplied by the service provider, such as cable companies supplying high-speed modems to subscribers willing to pay a monthly access fee of $40-50.[20] But, the equipment connecting a household to a shared facility is likely to be more closely tied to a particular technology. For example, a consumer might invest in cable that may be used to obtain high-speed wireline service, but is of little use when service is obtained from a wireless supplier.[21] As a result of this asset specificity, the household will not be in a good bargaining position with a wireless supplier. The cable will be a sunk investment that has little alternative use to the owner. The content supplier, knowing that the cable has limited alternative uses, will likely seek contractual terms that extract much of the value from the user.[22]

Notes

1. There is some possibility that high-speed access could be provided using the licensed and unlicensed Personal Communication Service (PCS) spectrum now allocated to paging and mobile telephony operations. Currently, however, most applications associated with this spectrum run at fairly low speeds. In such cases the high opportunity cost of using large bands of spectrum for high-speed data to the exclusion of many voice channels makes this an unlikely path for high-speed data access, at least in the near term. Over the longer term, unlicensed spectrum applications and improvements in wireless data protocols may solve this problem.

2. Kevin G. Wilson, "Canada's New Regulatory Framework: A Formula for Infrastructure Development?" Telecommunications Policy Research Conference, September 1996, p. 22.

3. For example, Kevin Wilson notes that the Canadian government has recently adopted policies that encourage cable and telephone companies to enter into each other's markets:

> Although I have found no explicit mention of it in the framework decision, it
> is reasonable to assume that it is grounded in the economics of infrastructure

development, or more appropriately, the *un*economics of infrastructure modernization. The CRTC's policy would appear to be grounded in the supposition that projected revenues from broadband common carriage will not be sufficient to foster investment in this technology. Ergo, the opening to common carrier participation in programming and other types of service content. Presumably, network operators will be able to justify investment in networks if they are allowed to benefit from revenues generated at the level of programming and other services carried over their networks. The presumption that network revenues will be insufficient to justify investment would appear to be born out by the slow growth of broadband implementation in the local loop. The CRTC's newfound tolerance of vertical integration in the telephone industry is clearly designed to create the most favorable conditions possible for investment in broadband technology. Ibid., p. 19.

See also Richard A. Cawley, "Adopting the European Union Telecommunications Regulatory Framework to the Developing Digital and Integrated Services Environment," Telecommunications Policy Research Conference, September 1996.

4. Milton Mueller, *Universal Service: Interconnection Competition and Monopoly in the Making of the American Telephone System* (Cambridge, MA, and Washington, DC: MIT Press/AEI Series on Telecommunications Deregulation, 1997), Chapter 5.

5. See, for example, Wisconsin State Telephone Association, *On the Line: A History of the Telephone Industry in Wisconsin* (Madison, WI: Wisconsin State Telephone Association, 1985), pp. 5, 10, 31, 44, 77, and 111; Constitution of the Kegonsa Independent Telephone Company, located in Minutes of the Board of Directors, Wisconsin State Historical Society (WSHS); and *Western Electrician* 16 (November 30, 1895), p. 267. A $25 expenditure in 1895 dollars is equivalent to about $320 in 1986 dollars. *Historical Statistics of the United States*, Vol. 1, p. 211; and United States Department of Labor, Bureau of Labor Statistics, *CPI Detailed Report: June 1986*, p. 28. Wisconsin's experience with rural telephony was not unlike developments in many other areas of the country, where the Bell system also refused to develop the rural market until it was faced with rivalry from locally financed telephone companies. These rural companies also relied on subscriber membership fees to finance the construction of the networks.

6. See, for example, Wisconsin State Telephone Association, pp. 8, 31, and 50; and Ettrick Telephone Company Records, General Telephone Company, Wausau, Wisconsin, p. 36.

7. In the early 1880s, it was the policy of American Bell to rely almost exclusively on local capital. The president of the company at the time, Forbes, believed that it was advantageous for the firm to have its stock owned by local people. This policy began to change around 1883 when the company concluded that it would be easier to connect different exchanges if they were under one management. Beginning in 1883, Bell started to consolidate operations into regional operating companies. Concurrent with this development, Bell exhibited a greater reliance on regional and national capital markets. Warren J. Stehman, *The Financial*

History of the American Telephone and Telegraph Company (Boston: Houghton Mifflin Company, 1925; reprint ed., New York: Augustus M. Kelley, 1967), pp. 37, 42–43.

The nascent era of rural telephony was also delayed as a result of Bell's refusal to sell its equipment to independent telephone companies. Rural communities were unable to obtain telephone equipment from independent manufacturers until Bell's patents expired. The failure of Bell to allow others to develop markets in which it had little or no interest was one of the high costs associated with the patent period.

8. By 1905, 10,000 of the 40,000 subscribers to Wisconsin Independent Telephone Companies were farmers. Most of these farmers belonged to roadline associations. *Proceedings of the Select Committee on Telephone Systems* (Ottawa: S.E. Dawson, 1905), Vol. 2, p. 121.

9. See, for example, Wisconsin State Telephone Association, pp. 4, 7, 11, 42, 60, 70, and 81; F.G. Johnson, "Experience of a Pioneer Physician in Northern Wisconsin," *Wisconsin Medical Journal* 38 (July 1939), p. 580; and Harry Barsantee, "The History and Development of the Telephone in Wisconsin," *Wisconsin Magazine of History* 10 (December 1926), p. 156.

10. See, for example, Wisconsin State Telephone Association; and Roy A. Atwood, "Telephony and Its Cultural Meanings in Southeastern Iowa, 1900–1917," (Ph. D. dissertation, University of Iowa, 1984), pp. 84, 117, 179, and 393. In Wisconsin, legislative policy aided the effort of these roadline and village companies to bring telephone service to the less densely populated areas of the state. In 1895, legislation was passed that granted these companies the right to construct their lines alongside public highways, provided that consent was first obtained from the appropriate public officials. George Mason Keith, "An Historical View of the Taxation of Telephone Utilities in Wisconsin," (Master's thesis, University of Wisconsin, 1931), p. 5.

11, Circular from Office of Wausau Telephone Company, February 16, 1897, Dane County Telephone Papers, WSHS (DCTP), p. 2; John A. Gaynor, letter to S. C. Thayer reprinted in Solon C. Thayer, "Telephone Service at Cost: The Wisconsin Valley Plan," pamphlet, 1905, p. 19; W. F. Goodrich, "Telephone Systems in La Crosse," *La Crosse Historical Sketches* (La Crosse, WI: La Crosse Historical Society, 1938), Vol. 4, p. 64; and letter from B. B. Clarke to Robert M. La Follette, August 30, 1895, DCTP. La Follette was one of the original financiers of the Dane County Telephone Company. In later years, while the governor of Wisconsin, he played a primary role in establishing the Railroad Commission.

12. J. C. Harper to William J. Bell, January 25, 1900; Bell to Harper, April 14, 1900; W. H. Buck to Harper, February 24, 1900; C. B. Salmon to William J. Latta, April 4, 1900, DCTP; and contract between Consolidated Telephone and Telegraph Company and People's Telephone Company, WSHS, series 1344, box 107, file 900.8.

13. General Accounting Office, "Telecommunications: Initiatives Taken by Three States to Promote Increased Access and Investment," March 12, 1996, GAO/RCED-96-68.

14. Kevin G. Wilson, "Canada's New Regulatory Framework: A Formula for Infrastructure Development?" Telecommunications Policy Research Conference, September 1996, p. 22.

15. Mueller, *Universal Service*, Chapter 3.

16. David Gabel, "Competition in a Network Industry: The Telephone Industry, 1894–1910," *Journal of Economic History* (September 1994), p. 548.

17. Farrell and Saloner have showed how uncertainty can delay the adoption of a new standard, even if the old standard is inferior. The same process that delays the adoption of a superior standard can also interfere with the deployment of new, improved facilities. Until a "bandwagon" effect develops, consumers are reluctant to embrace the new product. Joseph Farrell and Garth Saloner, "Standardization, Compatibility, and Innovation," *Rand Journal of Economics* 19 (1985) pp. 70–83.

18. See, for example, the description of the Net Day project in Connecticut, "'Barn-Raisin' to Wire Schools for the Internet," *New York Times*, August 22, 1996, p. B6. Net Days have been organized in all the continental states. As of October 1997, over 140,000 schools had reported to the Net Day organization that their schools had been wired for Internet access. See <http://www/netday.org>.

19. General Accounting Office, "Telecommunications: Initiatives Taken by Three States to Promote Increased Access and Investment," pp. 26–27.

20. "From Couch Potato to Cybersurfer," *Economist*, July 6, 1996, p. 72.

21. For example, Omoigui et al. report that in a fiber-to-the-curb architecture, a drop to a suburban home would cost $766, of which $407 (53 percent) is for labor. Nosa Omoigui, Marvin Sirbu, Charles Eldering and Nageen Himayat, "Comparing Integrated Broadband Architectures From an Economic and Public Policy Perspective," in *The Internet and Telecommunications Policy: Selected Papers from the 1995 Telecommunications Policy Research Conference* (Mahway, NJ: Lawrence Erlbaum Associates, 1996), p. 181. The labor cost would be a sunk cost that is essentially irreversibly tied in with use on a cable network.

22. This pricing practice takes place in the telephone switching market. Once a buyer makes a commitment to a vendor's product, the customer is locked in to the vendor. The switching equipment has proprietary protocols and interfaces that preclude or limit the ability of users to switch to other suppliers without changing their entire switch. Knowing this, the supplier is able to charge high prices for hardware and software after the initial switch is installed.

Delivering on the Promise: Scenarios for Deploying Local Access

Branko J. Gerovac and David C. Carver

How can we bring the kind of network connectivity enjoyed at larger institutions to homes, small businesses, schools, clinics, and other smaller enterprises? How can competing approaches be objectively evaluated? To aid such analysis, this chapter presents a set of criteria that incorporate the interplay of technology, business, and policy.[1] These criteria set the stage for discovering effective approaches that are technologically feasible, have viable business models, and advance public policy and social objectives.

A decade has passed since industry first promised to bring broadband communications to the home. Fiber to the home (FTTH) was then a favored approach, that is, until the cost of deploying a residential fiber infrastructure was taken into account. Since then, other well-known approaches have emerged. Yet, each time a particular approach gains favor, its deployment falls short. Either the technology does not scale and is overtaken by events or a viable business plan fails to emerge. In all cases, public policy issues, such as universal access and privacy, loom on the horizon.

In the early 1990s, the emphasis shifted to approaches that built on existing infrastructure. Integrated Services Digital Network (ISDN) was developed in the early 1980s for improved telephone service, but its use of digital modulation on existing copper wire led to its consideration for providing moderate bandwidth (64–128 Kbs) data service. Alternative technologies emerged, promising improved price, performance, and convenience. Cable modems offered high-bandwidth, Ethernet-style access overlaid on the hybrid fiber coax (HFC) cable television plant. When the World Wide

Web escalated Internet use, Asymmetric Digital Subscriber Line (ADSL), originally developed for video to the home, received increasing attention as a high-bandwidth copper wire alternative to cable modems.

Many of the approaches to interactive data communications, including ISDN, cable modem, and ADSL, divert technology that was developed largely for other purposes. Although it is appropriate to leverage existing infrastructure, such "bottom up" approaches may have inherited characteristics that put them at a disadvantage. Furthermore, given recent technological advances, it may again be time to consider new possibilities.

This chapter presents a subset of our criteria for analyzing alternative approaches to deploying high-bandwidth data services. It also includes a sample analysis that demonstrates the manner in which the criteria may be used to compare approaches that are already being implemented as well as to evaluate more speculative approaches, such as microcellular wireless. The real power of this criteria analysis is its utility in evaluating potential investment opportunities and risks.

Traditional Architectural Principles

Five criteria for analysis of alternatives to high-bandwidth data services represent traditional principles of communications architecture and design. These principles are fundamental to the Internet and were used, for example, in design and selection of the new digital television system. Approaches to providing high-bandwidth, local access to the Internet and other advanced communications services would also benefit from assessing the degree to which they incorporate and promote these principles.

Cross-industry harmonization. Since different communications industries have different strengths and liabilities, no one industry is able to deliver a complete solution. Thus, alternatives should be evaluated in terms of their ability to thrive in a mixed-industry marketplace. Successful approaches will likely derive essential strengths from practices across industries.

Digital technology. The computing, communications, and media sectors, including consumer electronics, are replacing their respective traditional analog technologies and adopting a common set of base digital technologies that potentially put local access on the "technology curve." Unfortunately, initial steps in the transition from analog to digital technology often apply analog systems design methodology to digital components, in an "analog bits" approach. Full incorporation of digital systems design methodology is required.

Open architecture and interoperability. Openness is the degree to which outside parties may contribute to creating and extending a system. Interoperability, in this context, is the extent to which a system may readily exchange data with other systems. Systems should be open in order to encourage competitive evolution of individual components and interoperable in order to ensure the efficient sharing of information (audio/video, voice, and data) across technologies, equipment, and services.

Extensibility. The pace of technological change demands that thought be given, in the initial design of a system, to accommodating unexpected future capabilities. Conversely, it is important not to ignore initial annoyances in a system that may be difficult to resolve later.

Scalability. Systems should function across a range of qualities and costs. Scalability is important to various aspects of the system: data stream transmission and reception, equipment price and performance, usage, provisioning, etc.

The above criteria have been accepted for such a long time that they are sometimes taken for granted or even forgotten entirely. In the competitive rush to develop high-bandwidth communications, these criteria are sometimes compromised in order to gain a false competitive advantage, which ultimately hurts both providers and their customers.

New Criteria

Criteria specific to the requirements of local access fit into three broad categories: technology; business models and markets; and policy and regulation. The following section briefly describes a representative subset of the local access criteria. While some of these criteria are occasionally mentioned in the popular press and technical discussions, it is usually in the context of promoting features of a particular approach. It is only by applying the criteria as a whole that the benefits and liabilities of different approaches may be revealed, thereby enabling meaningful comparisons across proposed alternatives.

Technology

Critical bandwidth steps. Critical bandwidth steps are levels in network access performance at which entire new classes of applications become possible, such as text versus voice versus video. Increases in bandwidth enable new classes of applications in a step-wise fashion. Thus, rather than measuring an approach by its bandwidth on a continuous scale, it is more important to consider the bandwidth step into which the approach generally falls and, therefore, the classes of application that it can readily support. The section below on ramifications further describes this factor.

Bandwidth symmetry. With symmetric service, the user can originate and receive data at roughly equivalent rates. With asymmetric service, bandwidth is received at a much higher rate than the rate at which it is originated. While asymmetric service may be deployed initially and may offer a substantial improvement over the kinds of service currently available, providers should consider when it will be technically feasible and competitively necessary to provide symmetric service and position themselves accordingly. Should the new infrastructure be designed to accommodate symmetry regardless of whether early deployment constraints warrant some degree of asymmetry, thereby anticipating a symmetric-ready system?

Peer-to-peer networking. Peer-to-peer networks permit direct access among equals on the network. All members of the network have access to the same capabilities and features. By contrast, "master-slave" networks require all access to be mediated by a master that has critical capabilities not available to the ordinary user. The Internet is inherently peer-to-peer. Telephone and cable systems are inherently master-slave. How will such inherited service structures be adapted to data communications? Are there new approaches that avoid this intrinsic contradiction?

Privacy, security, and network management. Sharing an infrastructure, especially an open one, with neighbors and local institutions exacerbates privacy, security, and network management problems. Failure to adequately address these issues will severely limit mass market deployment.

Mobility. People and their activities are becoming increasingly mobile, not tied to a particular office, building, or geographic location. Are there approaches that remove the hard distinctions between mobile, portable, and stationary services?

Product technology. Many component technologies, including microprocessors, memory, and mass storage, follow well-defined evolutionary curves, such as Moore's Law, which states that microprocessors tend to double in performance or halve in price every eighteen months. Local access is not yet on an evolutionary curve. Rather, it has improved in incremental fits and starts. Some approaches are a step in the right direction, others are not. For example, ISDN offers relatively low bandwidth with no clear path of improvement in price/performance. Symmetric, high-bandwidth cable modems are a step in the right direction and might even offer the kind of evolution seen in the development of 10 megabit, 100 megabit, and 1 gigabit Ethernet standards.

Business Models and Markets

Deployment realities. Existing and proposed local access systems should support incremental deployment and subsequent incremental upgrades and provisioning.

Capital investment. Investment models represented in the different scenarios need to be reconciled with various industries' business practices. For example, the telephone business has been oriented towards lengthy amortization schedules for infrastructure that is monolithic, costly to develop, and complicated to provision, whereas new infrastructure will be driven by rapid improvements (i.e., Moore's Law), short amortization, marginal pricing, and throw-away equipment.

Market transformation. Television, telephone, and computing as distinct services should give way to a new model in which the significant distinction is between content, communications, and interaction. Being on the technology curve means that acquiring a connection will be about bandwidth, not about function. Just as users choose the applications to run on their computer, they will have a wide range of choices about the ways that they use their communications connection, which will subsume traditional telephone, television, and data services.

Policy and Regulation

Regulatory regimes. Different industry approaches represent different regulatory regimes. Approaches that leverage traditional services and infrastructure have to contend with the associated traditional regulatory systems. How do the various approaches address regulatory issues? Do some approaches have advantages over others by virtue of their inherited regulatory regime? In any case, the single most important endeavor a government might undertake in this regard would be to set the ground rules and to articulate clearly the national policy objectives to be met in local access deployment. Otherwise, the massive private investment that is required will remain inherently risky and ineffective.

Ramifications

The criteria described above may have significant ramifications for proposed local access approaches when analyzed individually and in various combinations. For example, the criterion concerning critical bandwidth steps is based on the observation that bandwidth effectively comes in steps, each of which enables a new class of applications. This is referred to as the "1,3 Rule" because the steps roughly follow an exponential progression of 1, 3, 10, 30, 100, 300,... (see Figure 1).[2] Of course, there is some overlap from step to step, which are not hard and fast boundaries, but rules of thumb. The example in Figure 1 continues beyond 30 megabits per second to ever more demanding applications.

There is an important interplay between the critical bandwidth steps and the bandwidth symmetry criteria. Sooner or later, local access systems will commonly support video conferencing and allow users to originate graphically rich multimedia content directly from home servers. This threshold is estimated to be at roughly 3 megabits per second symmetric service, the point at which a user can both originate and receive any type of media that is in common use today. Exceeding 3 megabits per second becomes

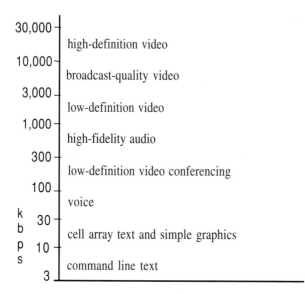

Figure 1 1, 3 Rule.

a matter of how many simultaneous transmissions can be accommodated.

This proposed level of service may seem exceedingly high, especially considering the limitations of current home equipment. Given the rapid pace of technological development, however, it is only a matter of time until this level of service becomes available. This sets the timeframe in which investments in interim approaches must show a return.

Sample Analysis

As an illustration, the following sections analyze and compare four deployment scenarios, using the criteria presented in this chapter. The four scenarios include:

Cable companies and cable modems. Cable has long been the bandwidth leader, considering the combined video, voice, and data traffic that it supports. For at least ten years, even before hybrid fiber coax technology, the coax cable plant has been touted as a vehicle for bringing high-bandwidth data communications to the home. Cable modems are attached at subscriber locations and at the cable plant head-end to create an Ethernet-style network shared by up to hundreds of users. The core technology was used in military communications more than two decades ago.

Telephone companies and ADSL. ADSL on the existing twisted-pair copper-wire plant, although originally oriented toward video on demand, is now being positioned as telephone companies' answer to the cable modem. Modems are attached to the phone line in the home and in the central office or neighborhood node to create a dedicated data link operating above the range of traditional voice signals. ADSL represents an important first step for the telephone companies' entry into consumer broadband services.

Fiber to the home. FTTH has always been seen as a future possibility, not yet cost-effective, but promised soon to become so. New fiber optic cable is deployed and optical transmitters/receivers create a link that is then aggregated with other links back to a central office switch. Since the introduction of cheaper transition technologies, such as cable modems and ADSL, fiber is not as prominent in discussions in the United States as it is in Japan, for example, where new fiber infrastructure is being installed.[3]

Microcellular wireless. This is a wildcard scenario. What if 20 channels of television spectrum—prime spectrum that goes through walls and buildings—were retired and reallocated for interactive data communications? What could be achieved? One result would be easy mobility and access across geographic locations in the same spectrum space. The technology to deploy a microcellular wireless service is within reach (e.g., spread spectrum, as discussed in the chapters by Hughes and by Beyer et al.), and may represent a high-leverage area of investment.

The ADSL and cable modems scenarios are compared across three technical and two business dimensions. Then the microcellular scenario is discussed, to show how the criteria may also be used to explore new alternatives. Table 1 summarizes this analysis, including FTTH, across the subset of criteria.

Technical Analysis

As the table shows, salient differences emerge across approaches when examining critical bandwidth steps and bandwidth symmetry. ADSL and some cable modem approaches are inherently

Table 1a

	Cable Modem	ADSL	FTTH	Microcellular
Critical Bandwidth Steps "1, 3 Rule"	10 Mbs down/ 10 Mbs up or 30 Mbs down/ 3 Mbs up (shared access, ~200 users)	Up to 8.192 Mbs down/640 Kbs up distance/line sensitive (dedicated line)	51 or 155 Mbs (fractional) (dedicated line)	Tens of Mbs within each cell (shared access)
Bandwidth Symmetry/ Asymmetry	Symmetric & range of asymmetric	Inherently asymmetric	Symmetric	Potentially symmetric
Privacy, Security, and Network Management	Shared link in neighborhood Hard to isolate catastrophic failures	Dedicated link more private and secure Slight regulatory advantage	Dedicated link	Shared link
Mobility	Speculative	NA	NA	Only cellular offers inherent mobility
Product Technology	Three-chip solution $40–100 Twice the cost per modem	Single-chip solution $20–50 Twice the number of modems	$30–50 loop fiber xmtr/rcvr	Undefined technology Expected costs comparable to cable modem
Deployment Realities	HFC promises a single plant for TV, telephony, and data Sharing limited	Initial deployment: upgrade DLCs, run new fiber where necessary (long term: FTTH) Crosstalk limited	Extensive initial build Local ordinances requiring buried new cable Cost limited	Initial cell sites Incremental cell subdivision Spectrum limited

Delivering on the Promise

Table 1b

	Cable Company	Telephone Company (xDSL)	FTTH	Microcellular
Capital Investment	Initial plant upgrade justified on improving CATV costs and service	85/15 rule: 85% of upgrade taken out of rate base (California formula) Largely self-financing	Massive up-front investment	Up-front spectrum auction cost
Market Transformation Broad shift to separating carriage and content Internet is inherently a nonbrokered service	Content broker History of content provider relationships A national broadcast infrastructure (high bandwidth)	Common carrier A national two-way long-haul infrastructure (Internet a "hostile" overlay on telcos' long-haul circuits)	Bundled brokerage and carriage rather than a universal bearer service	Potential for true peer-to-peer system
Regulatory Regime Transition from service-based monopolies to competition First Amendment rights with respect to the Internet	Content brokers Municipal regulation (Telecommunications Act raised questions)	Federal and state regulation Common carrier protection on First Amendment issues	Investment protection? Plant depreciation? Old regime: regulated monopoly	New regime Spectrum competition

asymmetric: the downstream channel is fairly high-bandwidth, but the upstream channel is relatively low-bandwidth, creating what could be termed an "interactive broadcast" service. Inherently symmetric applications, such as high-quality video conferencing that a grandparent would be comfortable using to view grandchildren, are thus precluded. Moreover, these approaches may also be inadequate for conducting business at home, thereby prolonging the anachronistic division between residential and business infrastructure and the associated large price disparity.

The critical bandwidth steps concept has important implications for services in which performance varies through a range of steps. ADSL performance is limited by crosstalk in the wire bundles and varies widely depending on wire length from the central office and line conditions. Cable modem performance is limited by the degree of sharing encountered at any given instant and thus can vary widely due to congestion. These are more than a "your mileage may vary" issue. Certain applications may work for your neighbor but not for you, or you may find you can look at video clips at 2:00 a.m. but not at 7:00 p.m.

Product technologies used in the different scenarios have advanced considerably in recent years. Just a few years ago, no practical solutions existed, but now a number of technologies are becoming cost-effective and viable. Still, none of them seems to offer a breakaway universal solution. Any of these technologies may be deployed as appropriate to a given situation, in light of population density, existing plant condition, competition, and economics. The prospect that multiple solutions will likely move forward raises important interoperability and portability issues.

Product technology will not be a substantial differentiator for ADSL and cable modems. ADSL technology is not as far along as cable modem technology, perhaps a generation or half a generation behind (perhaps 9–18 months), but it is catching up. ADSL modems might cost half as much as cable modems, but twice as many are needed in a deployment. Microcellular modems may be expected to follow the same cost curve as cable modems.

Business Analysis

This section examines capital investment and deployment realities across the selected scenarios and highlights the very different business models under which these industries operate.

Cable companies are generally debt-financed. Bankers usually try to justify new debt for system upgrades largely on the sales and maintenance of conventional cable television programming and services, rather than on speculative returns of untried services.[4] On this basis, cable companies are usually able to justify building a hybrid fiber coax plant servicing 2,000 homes per fiber node. Thus, at 10 percent penetration of a data service, a user effectively shares an Ethernet with 200 other potential users. An upgrade to 500 homes per fiber node can be achieved by supplementing node lasers and electronics; this will achieve 40 percent penetration with the same level of sharing. To improve this quality of service, the level of sharing must be reduced in some way, perhaps by charging more for the service thereby limiting penetration, by further subdividing the plant, or by adding channels.[5]

In contrast to cable companies, telephone companies are largely self-financed. Plant upgrades are primarily financed through increases in the rates for traditional services.[6] Since ADSL adapts to line conditions, its proponents claim potential deployment of up to an estimated 60 percent penetration.[7] Based on the estimated revenue to be generated at this higher level of penetration, telephone service and equipment suppliers claim that ADSL might be deployed initially on the existing wire plant, and then, as concentrations of communications traffic emerge, fiber connections might be expanded incrementally into the neighborhood, to the curb, and to the home.

Microcellular

New scenarios that exhibit more of the desired beneficial characteristics may also emerge. In the microcellular scenario, for example, retired television spectrum could be used to deploy a new data service. Digital television transmission, which is more spectrum efficient, promises to greatly enhance the services that broadcasters can offer and release a substantial portion of spectrum for new uses.

This approach might remove the operational partitioning between mobile, portable, and stationary systems. Many of the component technologies necessary to build a microcellular system already exist: wireless local area networks, packet radio networks, spread spectrum, and digital broadcast systems. Such a system could be symmetric capable and could easily offer shared access to tens of megabits per second within each cell. Microcellular product technology would follow cost curves similar to those for cable and ADSL modems. The number and size of cells would be scalable to permit incremental service deployment and upgrades and to optimize frequency reuse. Initially there would be a small number of cells, but subsequent cell subdivision would meet increased demand.

Television spectrum has a number of good transmission qualities, such as the ability to penetrate buildings, walls, and trees. In contrast, spectrum currently considered for data services is nonpenetrating and typically requires line-of-site transmission, thereby eliminating many of the desired benefits of wireless.

From a business perspective, this scenario requires significant upfront investments in developing technology, petitioning and lobbying the Federal Communications Commission (FCC) and Congress for spectrum allocations, and paying for auctioned spectrum licenses. Obviously, microcellular is speculative—perhaps even a long shot—but the potential payoff is substantial, making it a possible candidate for venture capital or the equity markets.

From a policy perspective, it is useful to draw a comparison to the origins of television. Fifty years ago, the federal government allocated a large chunk of high-quality radio frequency spectrum to provide free and universal access to television, then a nascent service. Clearly television has had an enormous impact on society. It was truly a high-leverage investment. Today, cable and satellite television systems are available, but universal access to free, over-the-air, terrestrial broadcast television is still considered critically important to promoting an informed citizenry.

What might the government do today to achieve a future payoff of this magnitude? Many of the arguments used 50 years ago and recast today for terrestrial broadcast television, such as its role in creating an informed citizenry, may also be applied to the creation of a wireless universal data service. Yet a universal data service would create not only an informed citizenry but also an involved citizenry. Thus it is certainly worth allocating high-quality spectrum to promote a national information infrastructure.

Recommendations

The full range of options for providing high-bandwidth local access services has yet to be adequately explored in the public forum. Even the brief analysis above suggests a few interesting observations. For example, it is clear that no single magic technology will be the all-around winner. Rather, a collage of technologies will be deployed in different settings, depending on local circumstances. Furthermore, microcellular wireless stands out as a new approach that addresses many of the criteria that other approaches neglect. Thus, microcellular wireless is also a worthy candidate for investment and national attention.

The sample analysis presented in this chapter was intended to be informative, rather than comprehensive. There are many additional criteria that contribute to a thorough analysis of local access. The results of such an analysis provide meaningful comparisons across proposed alternatives, offer competitive positioning of deployment scenarios, suggest transition strategies for existing systems, and encourage the creation of the conditions needed to deliver on the promise of local access to the information infrastructure.

Acknowledgments

This work was sponsored in part by the Defense Advanced Research Projects Agency and the National Science Foundation under contract NCR 9423889.

Notes

1. B. J. Gerovac and D. C. Carver, *Local Access to the Information Infrastructure*, Tutorial, Telecommunications Policy Round Table, September 1995; and B. J. Gerovac and D. C. Carver, *Local Access to the Information Infrastructure*, CIC America in the Age of Information, July 1995.

2. The "1, 3 Rule" corresponds approximately to a $10^{n/2}$ exponential progression.

3. Japanese Technology Evaluation Center, "Optoelectronics in Japan and the United States," study panel, February 1996.

4. "Money, Money, Money—Let's Do a Deal," panel session, NCTA Cable '96 Conference, April 30, 1996.

5. See "Quality of Service," B. J. Gerovac and D. C. Carver, in *Local Access to the Information Infrastructure*, CIC America in the Age of Information, July 1995.

6. For example, the California Public Utility Commission is allowing 85 percent of the upgrade cost to come from the rate base and requiring only 15 percent from new investments.

7. Kim Maxwell, chairman of the ADSL Forum, technical presentation on ADSL at the Federal Communications Commission, September 9, 1996.

The First 100 Feet for Households: Consumer Adoption Patterns

John Carey

Two important questions that must be addressed in building an advanced information infrastructure are: Do people want it, and will they pay to use it? Many analysts assume that new telecommunications technologies will succeed or fail in a marketplace context that is different from the markets for earlier technologies. A review of the history of technology introductions reveals, however, that many common factors affected the outcomes for those technologies. An understanding of these factors may inform the assessment of consumer responses to new technologies and services, such as interactive television, broadband Internet access, and advanced telephone services. Further, many historical lessons may be extracted from earlier marketplace experiences and applied to future technologies. This chapter reviews several common patterns associated with the adoption of earlier technologies and suggests ways in which these patterns may be used to support public policy planning for the National Information Infrastructure (NII), as well as for private sector technology and service development.

Pricing

The price of consumer electronic products has played an important role in determining the public's rate of adopting these products and the overall market size for them. Historically, products have been introduced at a high price in order to recover some of their research and development costs. Also, a company's early manufacturing of the product is generally expensive, since it cannot realize the economies of scale that are possible in mass production. Typically, the price drops sharply over time, spurring adoption by the mass public. Dozens of products have followed this pattern, including radios, black and white TVs, color TVs, and VCRs (see Table 1).

The same pattern has occurred with many telecommunications services. In 1910, the fee for basic telephone service in New York City was $20 per month[1] and the cost of a three-minute call between New York and Chicago in 1900 was over five dollars.[2] In 1997, the cost of basic telephone service in New York was $15 and the cost of a three-minute call between New York and Chicago was 45 cents.

A new technology must attract some early users who are able and willing to pay a high price for it, in order to achieve the economies of scale in manufacturing that reduce the price for the general public. Who purchases new products and services when they are expensive? The answer varies somewhat by product, but early purchasers are usually wealthy, have an insatiable desire for the product, or love electronic gadgets and are willing to pay a high price in order to be one of the first to own a new electronic device. Also, many early purchasers are businesses or schools that need the product.

The personal computer (PC), which is a core component of household access to advanced information services, has followed a different pricing pattern (see Figure 1). In the first phase of its history, rather than reduce the price of personal computers, manufacturers increased the capabilities of PCs each year. This was an appropriate response to the early market demand for PCs by business users and working professionals, who dominated house-hold usage. Consumers received the benefits of technological advances in the form of more speed and power, rather than a decline in price. In the past few years this pricing policy has changed, and adoption of PCs has increased sharply as the average price has approached $1,000.

It is also useful to note the price of these technologies at the point when they had entered half of U.S. households. These price points tell us when a median household decided that a new technology

Table 1 Average Price of Selected Electronic Products (Current Dollars)

Year	Radio Set	B&W TV	Color TV	VCR
1925	83			
1930	78			
1935	55			
1940	38			
1945	40			
1947		279		
1950		190		
1955		138	500	
1960		132	392	
1965			356	
1970			317	
1975			341	1,140
1980				1,122
1983				572
1985				494
1987				414
1989				382

Sources: Electronic Industry Association; Sterling and Haight; U.S. Department of Commerce.

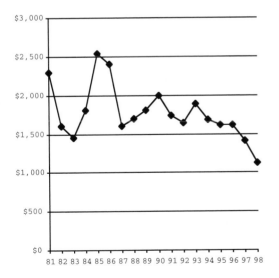

Figure 1 Average Price of Home Personal Computers, 1981–1998. Sources: Dataquest; Statistical Abstract of the United States.

Table 2 Number of Years to Reach a 50
Percent Penetration of U.S. Households

Technology/Medium	Years
Newspapers	100+
Telephone	70
Phonograph	55
Cable Television	39
Personal Computer	16*
Color Television	15
VCR	10
Radio	9
Black & White Television	8

*To reach 40 percent penetration.
Sources: Electronic Industry Association;
U.S. Dept of Commerce.

was affordable. Radio achieved a 50 percent penetration of U.S. homes in 1931, nine years after it was introduced. Black and white TV achieved a 50 percent penetration in 1955, eight years after it became readily available to the public.[3] Color television reached this level of penetration in 1972, and videocassette recorders achieved it at the end of 1987.

As of late 1997, personal computers had not yet entered half of U.S. households, and some research indicated that the growth rate for PCs was slowing down.[4] This apparent slowdown may have been related to price. For radio sets, black and white TV, and color TV, the technology cost approximately 1.8 or 1.9 weeks of household income when it reached a 50 percent penetration. The price of VCRs dropped to approximately one week's household income just before it had entered half of U.S. homes. If the cost and purchasing patterns for radio or TV apply, we would expect personal computers to achieve a 50 percent penetration rate at a price of $1,000 to $1,200, as in fact happened in early 1999. If the VCR model of price and purchase patterns is applicable, personal computers may have to decline to less than $750 dollars if they are to break through the 50 percent penetration level significantly and reach 60 or 70 percent.

Killer Applications vs. a Confluence of Factors

Those who develop and market new telecommunications technologies often herald "killer applications" and "magic bullets" that will lead to a decisive "home run" for a new technology or service. Indeed, there are examples of very popular applications that helped technologies to gain quick acceptance in millions of American homes. For example, a few very popular radio programs, such as *Amos n Andy,* drove the sale of radio sets.

More commonly, however, a confluence of several factors is required in order for a new communications technology to take off and gain widespread acceptance. Cable television and FM radio illustrate this pattern. Both were available to the public for many years before experiencing a period of rapid marketplace growth.

Cable television provides a useful illustration of the confluence process. In 22 years, from 1950 to 1972, cable television grew from zero penetration of U.S. households to 10 percent penetration. From 1972 to 1990, cable penetration jumped from 10 percent to just under 60 percent.[5] Why did penetration grow so rapidly in the 1970s and 1980s? In the 1950s and 1960s, cable television represented a way to improve television reception for communities with poor reception, generally small towns and suburban areas 50 or more miles from a broadcast transmitter. Cable offered very few extra channels or services, so it had little appeal in areas where there was good reception. In the 1970s, a confluence of several new elements acted as a starter motor for a large growth engine to kick in. First, Teleprompter Cable in New York City became profitable, which signaled to industry investors that large city cable systems were viable. At the same time, the Federal Communications Commission (FCC) lifted a freeze on franchise awards in major markets. In addition, satellite transmission made the distribution of national cable programs easier and less costly, which gave rise to the launch of many basic and pay channels, notably Home Box Office (HBO) and WTBS. Then, in the late 1970s, Warner Amex and Cox Cable became interested in interactive cable services. This encouraged much experimentation with program formats as well as investment in cable as the technology of the future.[6] The experimentation led to the development of several new channels with specialized pro-

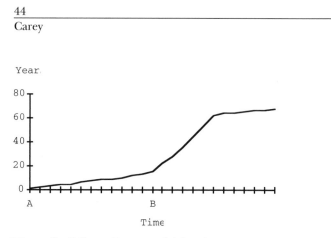

Figure 2 S-Curve Pattern of Adoption.

gramming, while the investment brought cable infrastructure to many communities that previously had no access to cable.

Cable television and other technologies slowly reached a threshold and then grew rapidly. This trajectory is often characterized as an S-curve pattern of growth, as shown in Figure 2. The elements required to reach the threshold will not be the same for all technologies and the timetable for reaching the threshold may vary by many years. Indeed, the crucial question associated with S-curves is the time required to move from launch of a new technology (Point A in Figure 2) to the threshold (Point B), where rapid growth begins. This period may vary from a few years to a few decades. Moreover, many technologies never reach the point at which rapid growth becomes possible, or they simply fail to gain marketplace acceptance.

Early and Later Uses and Users

The early uses and the early users of a technology may differ from later uses and later users. In other words, the market for a new telecommunications technology or service changes over time. A technology must attract a first group of users, if it is to survive long enough to attract a second group. Those who are introducing the technology should try to anticipate the mix of users and uses over time, but, since this is very difficult, they must be prepared to shift strategies based upon feedback from the marketplace.

VCRs illustrate this process. When VCRs were first introduced in the United States, they were quite expensive—approximately $1,500.

Businesses and schools that used the technology for training and education were early users, along with high-income households, especially those with an interest in the latest electronic gadget. Household use included taping television programs to view later (time-shift viewing) and watching pornography—a majority of videocassettes sold and rented in the late 1970s was pornography.[7] These uses made it possible for VCR prices to decline. The second wave of users tended to rent movies on videocassette and, later, to buy them.

This example suggests that there may be some services that might appeal to a mass market but never reach the mass market because no early group of users is prepared to pay the higher price or because of some other early barrier. In the case of VCRs, the unexpected emergence of "mom and pop" video rental shops was critical for mass adoption of VCRs. The growth of a technology is often a fragile, changing process.

Replacement Cycles and Pace of Change

The growth of some technologies is linked to the purchase of other technologies. For example, while few people in the 1980s bought a TV set or VCR just to obtain a remote control device or stereo sound, many consumers chose these features as options when they purchased a new VCR or replaced an old TV set. Thus, replacement cycles for existing technologies may provide an important opportunity to introduce new technologies. In U.S. households, color TVs are replaced after an average of eight years, telephone answering machines after five years, and personal computers after six years (see Table 3).

New models of an existing technology are purchased for at least four reasons: (1) to replace an existing model that no longer works; (2) to obtain an additional unit of the technology; (3) to upgrade an existing model that works but does not have a desired feature or is of lower quality than the upgrade model; or (4) as a byproduct of another purchase (e.g., a person may purchase a new personal computer that happens to come with a modem).

Upgrade purchases have been very important for technologies where the pace of technological change has been rapid, such as

Table 3 Replacement Cycles for Electronic Products

Product	Average Life (years)
Cordless Telephone	10
Color TV	8
Camcorder	7
CD Player	7
VCR	6
Personal Computer	6
Telephone Answering Machine	5
Fax	4

Source: Gannett News Service.

television and personal computers. For example, the percentage of households with both a personal computer and a modem grew from less than 10 percent in 1988 to more than 60 percent in early 1997.[8] The inclusion of modems in nearly all personal computers sold since 1994 helped this key peripheral device to cycle through the population of PC owners.

Failures, Fads, and Marketplace Decline

There are also many lessons to be derived from technologies that failed in the marketplace or lost ground after achieving a significant penetration of U.S. households. First, many technologies failed because they offered a superficial benefit. For example, quadraphonic sound, or four-channel sound, did not represent an advance in technology for the consumer market. Rather, it introduced an application of existing industrial technology (multitrack recording and playback) that provided a genuine industrial benefit (control of editing) into a home market where no benefit could be demonstrated. In addition, little software was developed for the new system, thus further reducing its appeal to consumers. From a consumer's point of view, quadraphonic sound offered no advantage over existing stereophonic sound. The failure of quadraphonic sound was predictable, but proponents ignored its weaknesses and instead tried to create advantages that were ephemeral.

Secondly, some technologies are fads. We are familiar with fads in leisure products, such as hula hoops, yo-yos, and pet rocks. Similarly, consumer electronic technologies and services may also be fads or have a fad component. For example, in the early 1970s, citizen's band (CB) radio had a steady population of approximately 200,000 users. As CB became a fad in the mid-1970s, the population of users grew to a peak of 10 million in 1976. It then declined rapidly and leveled off at approximately one million users by the early 1980s.[9] More recently, CB radio has experienced another surge in use by immigrants who are using it as a substitute for long-distance telephone calls. It remains unclear whether this is another fad or if this group of users will adopt CB as a long-term service.

Third, some technologies experience cyclical patterns of strong adoption, decline in usage, and periodic returns to popularity and usage. For example, 3-D movies were very popular during the mid-1950s, then faded away, but experienced renewed interest in the 1960s and for brief periods in each decade thereafter. Videogame consoles and associated software surged in the early 1980s, collapsed in the mid-1980s, and were resurrected in the late 1980s. In the 1990s, videogames experienced cyclical growth and decline, although not as extreme as in the 1980s. These peaks and valleys have been associated with the introduction of new generations of equipment, which fade in popularity after a few years. More recently, PC videogames have begun to compete with console videogames, leading to another dip in videogame console hardware and software sales, even though a new generation of technology was introduced in 1996. But, the decline has not been as precipitous as the decline in the mid-1980s.

Sometimes, an apparent failure is merely a false start. For example, television was launched as a commercial service in the late 1930s, but the high price of TV sets ($600) and the disruption caused by World War II led to a halt in service.[10] The technology was reintroduced after World War II and grew rapidly. Similarly, two home video recording technologies, the EVR system by CBS and Avco's Cartrivision system, were launched and then withdrawn in the early 1970s, before the modern VCR finally took hold in the mid-1970s. Fax technology wins the prize for false starts. It was invented in the 1840s and tested in the 1860s with no significant adoption, reintroduced unsuccessfully in the 1930s and the 1950s, achieved widespread adoption in the business market during the 1970s, and finally entered large numbers of households in the 1990s.[11]

Enhancements and New Services

It is useful to distinguish enhancements to existing technologies from the development of entirely new services. Qualitative enhancements to existing technologies often provide a good path for the development of many new telecommunications technologies. Consumers have responded positively to enhancements, such as adding color to black and white television, higher fidelity for recordings, stereo sound for television, and touchtone telephone service. From a supply-side perspective, consumers were adopting new technologies and services. From a demand-side perspective, consumers were simply upgrading to a better version of a familiar and desirable technology or service.

New services, by contrast, provide a more radical change from earlier services and often include new content. Examples include new cable channels, personal computer software, video games, and electronic mail. In addition, new services often add higher costs than enhanced services, especially if they involve the creation of content. New services also require a change in the way that people use media. For example, a person watching color television uses the same content as someone watching black and white television, even though there is a qualitative difference in their experience. In contrast, someone watching basic cable channels for the first time in the 1970s or participating in a telephone conference call in the 1980s was altering his behavior. This kind of change is more significant because it requires people to alter existing media habits. Such a change often requires time. Indeed, the growth in use of basic cable channels and the rise in use of electronic mail spanned a number of years.

A related issue is the demand for new or enhanced services. Many analysts have noted that new technologies are often created by engineers who have little knowledge about whether there is a demand for the technology.[12] In this sense, new services often result from "technology push," rather than user demand. This phenomenon has been cited as a reason for the failure of many technologies. Yet, most communications technologies introduced in the twentieth century, such as motion pictures, radio, phonographs, and television, entered the marketplace in a context of uncertain demand. Technologies do not falter simply because they represent technology push. They fail because they cannot meet the challenge of finding or creating applications that people want.

Who controls content creation for a new technology? Sometimes a new group of entrepreneurs leads content development, as has been the case with early personal computer software and much of the early content on the World Wide Web. In other instances, existing players control content for the new technology, as with compact discs (CDs), which are produced by the same industry that created record albums and audiocassettes. Entrepreneurs are more likely to bring creativity to the process and to generate new ideas, while existing players are more likely to bring financial resources and organizational relationships and to help ensure that the technology has a reasonable opportunity to succeed in the marketplace.

Applying Historical Lessons to the Adoption of Advanced Telecommunications Technology

The preceding review of consumer adoption patterns for earlier telecommunications technologies and services suggests several lessons that may provide guidance about the manner in which consumers are likely to respond to advanced data, video and telephony services. The first lesson is general: the technology used in delivering a service is far less important to an ordinary consumer than the service itself. It is important, therefore, to place an emphasis on the services that will be delivered by an advanced telecommunications infrastructure, rather than on the way they will be delivered. Similarly, consumers may not distinguish services in terms of the bandwidth required to deliver a service. Consumers are certainly able to distinguish a dial-up sports score service over the telephone from a video sports segment on a PC or TV. They are more likely to think, however, about the advantages of convenient access, timeliness of information, and the fun of watching video clips of games than the bandwidth of the distribution channel. More generally, it is important to think in simple terms about the motivations and desires of end-users. Many discussions of broadband networks focus on comparative engineering benefits or economic advantages for suppliers of services. End-users, such as residential customers, are often taken for granted in the planning of advanced networks. Instead, the focus should be on end-users—consumers who are able to take the initiative and adopt new technology—and the presentation of new services in an appealing way.

Positive Indicators

There are many positive indicators of consumer interest in services that will utilize an advanced telecommunications infrastructure. The first of these is spending patterns. After decades of relatively constant spending on media and information as a share of household income,[13] consumers increased their spending steadily throughout the 1980s and 1990s. Table 4 shows the growth in total consumer electronics spending between 1992 and 1997. Further, early adopters in the 1990s have spent heavily on a range of telecommunications and entertainment services, as shown in Table 5.

In addition, there has been a sharp increase in the number of households subscribing to online and Internet services, as shown in Figure 3. It appears that the use of these services may have reached a critical threshold. It is unclear how high penetration will rise or when growth will begin to level off.

The growth in online subscriptions has been accompanied by a growth in second telephone lines within households and a general trend toward multiple units for technologies, such as televisions, radios, telephones and personal computers.[14] This indicates an increased demand for existing services as well as more personalized use of technologies, for example, a teenager talking on one phone line while a parent talks on another. In turn, it suggests that consumer demand for an advanced telecommunications infrastructure may be linked to an aggregation of existing and new

Table 4   Consumer Spending on Electronic
Media, 1992–1997

Year	Total Spending (billions of dollars)
1992	47
1993	52
1994	58
1995	63
1996	66
1997	70

Source: Consumer Electronics Manufacturers
Association.

Table 5   Spending on Information and Entertainment by Early Adopters,
1996

Technology or Service	Range in Spending per Year ($)
Cellular Phone Service	625–675
Local Phone Service	475–525
Long-Distance Phone Service	375–425
Cable or Satellite TV	350–400
Newspapers/Magazines	300–350
Paging	225–275
Online/Internet	175–200
Information Hardware	200–250
Entertainment Hardware	375–425
Videocassette Rentals/Purchases	200–300
Total Spending	3,000–3,500

Sources: American Demographics; Anderson Consulting; *Wall Street Journal.*

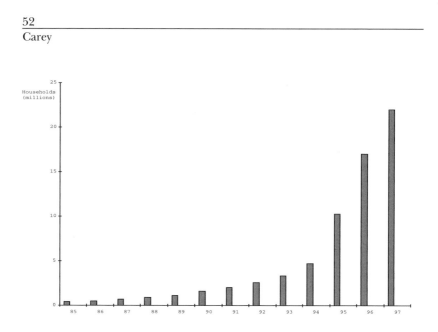

Figure 3   Number of U.S. Households Subscribing to an Online or Internet Service Provider, 1985-1997. Source: Veronis & Suhler; Jupiter Communication.

services, such as a package of multiple telephone lines and a high-speed data line.

Target Early Adopters

A review of adoption trends for earlier technologies suggests that there are three important groups of early adopters. The first comprises technophiles who feel compelled to have the latest electronic gadgets and "hot rod" delivery systems. They are largely males with higher incomes. The second group consists of households with home offices and includes people who operate businesses from their homes, telecommuters who work part-time at home and part-time at a regular office, and workers such as teachers or lawyers who maintain an office at home to complement their regular place of work. The number of home offices has grown sharply, from approximately 20 million in 1988 to more than 33 million in 1997.[15] Households with home offices typically adopt new telecommunications technologies earlier than other households. For example, in 1996, 42 percent of telecommuters had two or more telephone lines, compared to 17 percent of all households, and 37 percent had a fax machine, compared to 11 percent of all households.[16] Curiously, there has been relatively little marketing of advanced telecommunications services, or even added capacity, to consumers with home offices. Advertising for high-speed digital phone lines (ISDN) or even second telephone lines has been sparse.

The third group of early adopters consists of households with moderate or high income and children. More than 60 percent of households with a computer also have children under 18 present. Many parents believe that their investment in information technology and services will help their children to do better in school and to find better jobs in the future. Children also have shown a strong interest in computers, although this may be as much for entertainment as education. Personal computers are the second most requested item on the Christmas lists of American children.[17]

The business and education sectors are important target groups that may lead to consumer adoption of advanced telecommunications services. In the past, many technologies entered businesses and schools first, creating habits and appetites that people eventually brought home. For example, the telephone was predominantly a business service in the late nineteenth century. It later entered households of business people who wanted the same service at home. Similarly, many people developed an appetite for the personal computer in business or educational settings, then brought it into their homes.

Motivations and Desires

Why do consumers adopt new technologies and services? A good starting point is consumers themselves and their behavior. One useful historical example that should not be followed is provided by the early Bell System. For decades, the Bell System marketed telephones to consumers as serious business tools in the home and actually discouraged uses of the telephone for social chatting or casual conversations among family members. It was well into the twentieth century when Bell marketing efforts recognized and reflected how people were actually using the telephone.[18]

Among the more important motivations to adopt new technology and services is a strong need. A consumer has an existing unmet need, a new service meets the need at an acceptable cost, and the consumer adopts the service. There are many examples of new technology adoption based upon need. For example, when home satellite dishes cost $2,000 to $3,000 in the 1980s, they were adopted by 20–25 percent of households in western states, such as Montana and Idaho, where there were few local broadcast signals or cable systems. In the current context, candidate unmet needs include services that support work at home and multimedia education services for children and adults, such as recertification courses for harried professionals.

A second motivator is an insatiable appetite for some content or service. For example, gadget lovers will pay just about any price for the latest technology and many people cannot consume enough of some content, such as movies, soap operas, or pornography. Often, consumers with insatiable appetites add the new technology or service to the old, rather than substitute the new for the old. In the current context, candidate "insatiables" are much the same as they have been in the past.

Inconvenience is a notable third motivation for adoption and change. Many models of change are based upon positive motivations, but painful experience with an existing service can provide an incentive to adopt new services. In planning advanced telecommunications services, it may be useful to ask: Where are consumers experiencing inconvenience or bad service delivery that might be relieved by a high-capacity telecommunications infrastructure? Possible answers include slow Internet access, low stocks of popular movies in video rental shops, and poor customer service by existing broadband service providers.

Supplier pressure can lead to adoption and change, but it can also backfire. That is, suppliers of services may have sufficient control over a market to force consumers to change behavior. For example, a bank that dominates a local market might increase the price of all services provided by tellers and thereby motivate consumers to make greater use of automated teller machines (ATMs). However, in a competitive telecommunications environment, it is not clear whether such a strategy would work.

The marketplace for advanced multimedia services is changing rapidly. The motivations and wants of Internet users are also changing as a mass market is emerging. While the early users of the Internet included mostly well-educated information seekers, the Internet is now attracting a mass market of people with mixed educational backgrounds, younger and older users, and more people who are looking for entertainment. Communication still remains the anchor for Internet use.[19] It is important for planners to think about the future evolution of the Internet, rather than its past.

Conclusion

What does this review of historical trends imply for telecommunications policy and the planning of the National Information Infrastructure, as well as for private sector technology and service development? For policymakers, history suggests that it is very difficult to know with precision the applications and services that will emerge successfully after the NII is in place. The development of the telephone network, assignment of spectrum for radio and television, franchising of cable systems and development of the backbone for the Internet were all undertaken with only a weak understanding of the services that would succeed. Telecommunications policy should support the development of an advanced information infrastructure as an investment in the future, not as a blueprint for the future.

Since the future is unpredictable, telecommunications policy must also support flexibility for service providers as they develop applications, discover that they are off course, and seek to adjust service offerings or to create new ones. When teleports were first designed, the thinking was that the core of the business would be city-to-city transportation of data and other services via satellite. In order to reach the satellite uplinks, fiber-optic rings were built around business districts. Through serendipity, the fiber-optic rings became the core of the business for teleports, moving data and other services at high speeds within cities. Many services for consumers that utilize the NII may also miss the mark initially and should be allowed the flexibility to change.

Telecommunications policy should also support broad consumer access to services delivered via the NII. Ideally, all homes will have access to advanced telecommunications services via the NII within a short time frame. A review of historical patterns, however, indicates that this has rarely been achieved. Many technologies have been used by businesses first, then by certain consumers and wealthy households before being adopted by the mass public. A more realistic policy may be to support broad public access to NII services, but to ensure access through public location terminals. Examples include public telephone booths in the first quarter of the twentieth century and, more recently, computers in public schools and Internet access terminals in public libraries.

For private sector developers, there is ample evidence of strong consumer demand for services delivered via the NII. Consumers will invest in the first 100 feet, if services meet existing needs or create a demand for exciting new products. Communication and entertainment are likely to be the anchors that drive demand. Information and transactions need to be targeted to groups with specific needs and wants, such as harried working professionals, people who work at home, and parents with school-age children.

Acknowledgements

Research for this chapter was supported by the Media Studies Center of the Freedom Forum Foundation.

References

Erik Barnouw, *The Golden Web: A History of Broadcasting in the United States 1933–1953* (New York: Oxford University Press, 1968).

Claude Fischer, *America Calling: A Social History of the Telephone to 1940* (Berkeley, CA: University of California Press, 1992).

A. Michael Noll, *Highway of Dreams: A Critical View Along the Information Superhighway* (Mahway, NJ: Lawrence Erlbaum Associates, 1997).

Ithiel de Sola Pool, ed., *The Social Impact of the Telephone* (Cambridge, MA: MIT Press, 1977).

Jerry Salvaggio and Jennings Bryant, eds., *Media Use in the Information Age: Emerging Patterns of Adoption and Use* (Hillsdale, NJ: Lawrence Erlbaum Associates, 1989).

Christopher Sterling and Timothy Haight, *The Mass Media: Aspen Institute Guide to Communication Industry Trends* (New York: Praeger Publishers, 1978).

U.S. Department of Commerce, *Historical Statistics of the United States: Colonial Times to 1970* (Washington, DC: Bureau of the Census, 1975).

Notes

1. Ithiel de Sola Pool, ed., *The Social Impact of the Telephone* (Cambridge, MA: MIT Press, 1977), p. 130.

2. U.S. Department of Commerce, *Historical Statistics of the United States: Colonial Times to 1970* (Washington, DC: Bureau of the Census, 1975), p. 784.

3. Christopher Sterling and Timothy Haight, *The Mass Media: Aspen Institute Guide to Communication Industry Trends* (New York: Praeger Publishers, 1978), pp. 367–373.

4. Jared Sandberg, "PC Makers' Push into Homes May Be Faltering," *The Wall Street Journal*, March 6, 1997, p. A12.

5. Dan Brown and Jennings Bryant, "An Annotated Statistical Abstract of Communications Media in the United States," in Jerry Salvaggio and Jennings Bryant, eds., *Media Use in the Information Age: Emerging Patterns of Adoption and Use* (Hillsdale, NJ: Lawrence Erlbaum Associates, 1989), pp. 292–293.

6. Lee Becker, "A Decade of Research on Interactive Cable," in William Dutton, Jay Blumer, and Kenneth Kraemer, eds., *Wired Cities: Shaping the Future of Communications* (Washington, DC: The Washington Program of The Annenberg School of Communication, 1987), pp. 102–123.

7. Bruce Klopfenstein, "The Diffusion of the VCR in the United States," in Mark Levy, ed., *The VCR Age: Home Video and Mass Communication* (Newbury Park, CA: Sage Publications, 1989), pp. 21–39.

8. See Veronis, Suhler & Associates, *Communications Industry Forecast* (New York: Veronis, Suhler & Associates, 1996), p. 317; and Odyssey Homefront Survey, cited in CSS Internet News, March 12, 1997.

9. John Carey and Mitchell Moss, "The Diffusion of New Telecommunications Technologies," *Telecommunications Policy* (June 1985), pp. 145–158.

10. Erik Barnouw, *The Golden Web: A History of Broadcasting in the United States 1933–1953* (New York: Oxford University Press, 1968), pp. 125–128.

11. Ibid., p. 115; and Catherine Rubio Kuffner, "Legal Issues in Facsimile Use," *Media Law And Policy* 5, No. 1 (Fall 1996), p. 8.

12. A. Michael Noll, *Highway of Dreams: A Critical View Along the Information Superhighway* (Mahway, NJ: Lawrence Erlbaum Associates, 1997), pp. 96–97.

13. Maxwell McCombs and Chain Eyal, "Spending on Mass Media," *Journal of Communication* 30, No.1, pp. 153–158.

14. Statistical Research Inc., SMART Home Technology Survey, 1996.

15. Susan Wells, "For Stay-Home Working, Speed Bumps on the Telecommute," *The New York Times*, September 17, 1997, p. 1.

16. Find/SVP Survey, cited in *USA Today*, November 25, 1996, p. 2B.

17. Consumer Electronics Manufacturers Association survey, cited in *Video Business* (December 1995), p. 58.

18. Claude Fischer, *America Calling: A Social History of the Telephone to 1940* (Berkeley, CA: University of California Press, 1992), p. 161.

19. James Katz and Philip Aspden, "Motivations for and Barriers to Internet Use," Telecommunications Policy Research Conference, Solomon Islands, Virginia, October 6, 1996; and Robert Kraut et al., "The HomeNet Field Trial of Residential Internet Services," *Communications of the ACM* 39, No. 12 (December 1996), pp. 55–65.

Models for Bottom-Up Investment

The Local Wireless Option

David R. Hughes

Advances in digital signal processing for wireless data radios have opened up new possibilities for local Internet access. One of the most appealing forms of wireless is spread spectrum data radio technology, which requires no license to operate in the United States. This chapter will begin by reviewing several compelling reasons why this technology may help build a ubiquitous telecommunications infrastructure at the local level. It will then describe current market and regulatory factors that might limit this opportunity. The chapter will conclude with a recommended regulatory approach for capturing the social and market potential of spread spectrum.

The case for spread spectrum may be summed up in four points. First, the radio technology of spread spectrum can theoretically scale to millions of radios and users, sharing spectrum even in a congested urban environment. This is contrary to historical limitations of analog radio communications of the past, when radios using one dedicated slice of the spectrum would interfere, or be interfered with, by other radio transmissions in the same frequency range. Many digital radios using spread spectrum techniques can operate in the same space as other, like radios, without effective interference.

Secondly, spread spectrum technology can minimize or eliminate radio "interference." The U.S. Federal Communications Commission (FCC) is able to write rules that permit transmission of signals without users being required to get licenses, or numbers, in a particular location. Only the design of the radios have to be licensed by the FCC to ensure that they meet minimum spread spectrum technical specifications that limit interference. Spread spectrum radios may then be used anywhere, including as mobile connections. They are ideally suited for relatively short range connectivity, such as to the nearest Internet point of presence, bypassing the telephone company. They thus may become a "capital expenditure only" connectivity solution, rather than a "capital expenditure plus recurring local loop cost" model.

Third, the development of a range of such digital radios over the past 12 years has demonstrated the possibility for the data radio industry to offer devices and some commercial services based on them, which are affordable to individuals as well as end-user organizations.

Finally, the combination of the above characteristics—noninterfering, no-license, shared spectrum, affordable digital radios—opens the door to entirely new business models for communications. Digital radios allow a new "device" model, where the cost is in the radios as devices, and there is no communications charge, rather than the "service" model, where the customer pays for the communications service, while the equipment is incidental. This model challenges the telephone company model, allowing customers to buy spread spectrum radios to connect up their computers to neighbors, their offices, schools, or the Internet, and pay no telephone company charges.

While the price and performance of wireless access to data networks now in use compared favorably with commercial wired solutions for any bandwidths higher than dial-up modem speeds, acceptance has been inhibited by a lack of working knowledge about wireless spread spectrum technology. In addition, there are strong vested interests favoring wired access solutions. The combination of ignorance and resistance has retarded the development of wireless data communications as a mass market solution to lower the costs and improve the technical performance of local connectivity to the Internet.

Lobbying pressure from the telephone companies, in this era of growing business in connecting people to the Internet, has influenced the FCC to limit the frequencies that spread spectrum radios may use and the power that they may generate. These restrictions in turn limit their effective range, often to distances of less than 20 miles, such that radios must maintain "line of sight between radios" positioning with respect to one another. Spread spectrum technology itself is not limiting, but the rules under which it may operate are.

Analog, Digital, and Spread Spectrum Transmissions

The most fundamental change that has made digital wireless a possible solution is the dramatic increase in the processing power of digital signal processors—computer chips—over the past 25 years, along with equally dramatic falling prices and the substantial miniaturization of devices using such chips. These advances have permitted the digitization of radio transmissions as well as a corresponding ability to detect such signals and to distinguish them from noise at ever lower levels of radiated power. Earlier radio, current general television, and even most current cellular telephone signaling is analog, not digital. And the experiences of people attempting to use analog cellular phones or traditional narrow-band analog radio systems for data or web access have shown how poor such analog radio devices are for local Internet access. But digital access, using entirely new techniques now permitted by the FCC, is changing that picture.

The radio engineer, Paul Baran, has explained that analog signals, such as those used in television, need exclusive slices of spectrum because, even if an "interfering" signal is only 1/10,000 as strong as the TV signal, there would be visible TV image disturbance. But, if the signal is digitized, that interfering signal may be 1,000 times stronger without causing visible interference. In other words many, many more radios, televisions, cell phones, and computer communications can coexist in the same electromagnetic space, without effective interference from digital signaling, than is possible with analog signaling.

Spread spectrum is a highly promising form of digital transmission for providing broadband access to the Internet. Spread spectrum uses digital signal processors to disassemble a stream of data fed into the radio from a source computer. The data is broken down to the sub-byte level. It is bundled in digital form into tiny packets of data. The radio transmits those packets in short bursts in random ways over a wide range of frequencies at very low levels of power. (Thus "spread" spectrum.) A corresponding radio at the other end, using the same proprietary algorithms together with one of a number of ways to synchronize its reception of the patterns used by the first radio, captures and analyzes the packets, retries for lost packets if necessary, reassembles the packets, and feeds them into a receiving system, computer, or network.

The error-correcting techniques possible for digital signaling are able to deal robustly with any interference that does occur. If a great deal of interference occurs, the usual effect is that the rate of data exchange slows down, from retrying to get the signal through perfectly, rather than fails completely.

Since the transmissions are being generated by proprietary systems, they may only be intercepted with the greatest difficulty. For even greater security, the messages may be encrypted. One technique commonly used is for each radio in a network to have its own encoded identifying number and for every packet of data that is encoded by the processor to contain that target, as well as origination, address. When the radio for which the transmissions are intended examines the flood of background noise and transmissions from other radio sources, including other spread spectrum radio sources, the receiver processes and passes through only the transmissions that are addressed specifically to it by number, according to the proprietary algorithms contained in each radio.

Interception of these radio patterns requires simultaneous monitoring of a large number of frequencies and capture of all the data. Radios and systems attempting to intercept the intelligent information flow receive, therefore, huge amounts of intermixed data and noise. It is then necessary to sort out the intelligent information from all emanations issuing from other sources in the same band of frequencies, to order it in the sequences sent, and to decode it by substantial processing power. As a result, spread spectrum transmissions are surprisingly secure, even without encryption. In fact, spread spectrum was developed by the U.S. military in order to permit clandestine global and battlefield communications that could not be effectively intercepted or jammed.

One advantage of using spread spectrum radios for providing Internet access is its scalability. Many radios can use the same frequencies at the same time without noticeably impairing the quality of service. Spread spectrum, using fast frequency hopping or direct sequence, or hybrid techniques, over very wide spectra, and transmitting with low power, can coexist with other radios using the same frequencies or bands. How many radios can operate in the same space? One recent study from MIT explains that "the overall noise level in the system...is found to be manageable even as the system scales to billions of nodes."[1] Engineers, regulators, and businesspeople will argue whether these kinds of results are really attainable in the real-world marketplace.

There is no practical limit to the numbers of radios that may coexist in the same electromagnetic space. The capability of a pattern of radios designed and laid out according to the study cited above exceeds the number of people per square mile in densely populated cities. In other words, the capability exceeds the likely maximum number of radios and users in the practical world. But it is a chicken-and-egg proposition, involving the way that the FCC makes the rules both to enable and to encourage radio manufacturers to build profitable radio businesses. Exploring the limits of the technology will require research and development, which will occur only if FCC rules encourage market development of the technology.

While no system has approached such a large system of users, the claims of early digital radio firms are impressive. For example, Omnipoint, which received a Pioneer Preference Award spectrum allocation from the FCC, claims that their most advanced spread spectrum wireless network technology can accommodate 490,000 users per square mile. This assertion means that its technology may be deployed at one tenth the cost of analog cell phones, as a result of the much higher density per "cell" made possible by the increased efficiency of its spread spectrum based cell phone technology.

The Government Spectrum Rules

The 1985 FCC rules governing spread spectrum radios require that radios using spread spectrum methods of management must share spectrum in what are called the Part 15—Industrial, Scientific and Medical—no-license bands. These are the bands in which devices from microwave ovens to cross-room cordless phones to audio speaker systems operate. Some call them the "garbage bands" of telecommunications. These bands are in the 915 MHz, 2.4 GHz, and 5.8 GHz ranges of the spectrum. The radios must be certified and meet certain technical specifications, such as the number of spread spectrum hops they may employ, and they must specify the limits of transmitter power, one watt being the current level, and the antenna gain[2] that may be permitted.

Despite these limitations and the resistance of U.S. intelligence agencies, more than 60 companies have produced spread spectrum, no-license radio devices, aimed largely at the corporate marketplace for high-bandwidth, short range, urban deployments. These products provide a range of data connections from 10 Mbps very short range wireless LANS, through a variety of medium speed (56 to 115 kbps), wireless "modems," to high speed (1.5 to 2 Mbps) T-1 class radio "bridges" operating reliably and securely up to 25 miles per "hop." A company called Solectek has even announced a 25 mile, 10 Mbps spread spectrum digital radio that operates under the severely restricted rules of the FCC for such radios, which is essentially no more than one watt of transmitted power and four watts of EIRP of antenna gain. The radios, so far aimed at large organizations, cost from $1,500 to $10,000 and are, therefore, not yet end-user commodity priced devices, where the first 100 feet problem is most acute. This situation is changing rapidly. In order to stimulate the development of lower-cost radios, the National Science Foundation has awarded a $1 million grant to the Tucson Amateur Packet Radio (TAPR), a digital branch of American amateur radio (HAM), to produce a prototype radio. This radio will deliver T-1 wireless speeds, in ranges from 10 to 200 kilometers depending on allocated frequencies for use, and cost less than $500 for the end product.

New Options

No-license digital wireless implies no commercial service. In a license-free environment, the spectrum is effectively a public, nonproprietary good. The primary cost of a wireless connection is the purchase, installation, and maintenance of digital radios between a point of presence, or between points within an organization, building, or neighborhood, rather than a per minute or per month service charge. Wireless requires no costly infrastructure, rights-of-way, or maintained wires, so its ongoing costs are lower than for telephone or cable services.

There is no requirement that no-license radio be free. Indeed, there are several instances of companies using the Part 15, no-license radios to provide telco-bypass, commercial services that can operate above the standard 28.8 kbps wired modem rate. Metricom, of Los Gatos, California, provides, in Cupertino, California, Seattle, and Washington DC, a spread spectrum digital wireless service. Individuals buy or lease Richochet wireless modems to connect to the serial ports of their computers and, for $30 a month, have unlimited cross-town use of bandwidth. While the radios are rated at 77 kbps, realistically, with the load on the pole top antennas deployed across the town, the rates are from 28.8 kbps to a best case of 56 kbps.

The same wireless modems, connecting to each other in pairs, can communicate from a quarter-mile up to a mile in best cases at a nominal 56 kbps, point to point. One modem may be put into the serial port of a server and the other modem into the port of the user's computer and free, secure, error-free communications may take place between the user's computer, the port on the server, and then out to any destination linked to the server.

Such spread spectrum-based wireless modems may also be used to create patches to locations that do not have telephone connections. A pair of wireless modems, along with a 28.8 kbps phone modem and a null cable adapter, have been put in conference rooms or at podiums that are not served by a telephone line. By attaching the first wireless modem to the computer at the point of work and the second modem near the closest outside telephone line and then connecting the wireless modem to the wired modem with a null cable, it becomes possible to patch the telephone line to the work computer at no cost to, at least, the nearby server. These patches may be implemented in an apartment complex, a school system, a business office complex, without even internal LAN wiring. The modems, which are not designed specifically for such purposes, sell at retail for approximately $595. If purchased as part of a municipal or campus commercial service, the price is closer to $300 each. Such improvised patches demonstrate the potential for the development of wireless modems for very local portability, without the corresponding costs of cellular telephones.

Free Wave of Boulder, Colorado, offers a higher-bandwidth, longer-range product line, which may be used as a substitute for both a modem and a wireless network. It illustrates yet another set of possibilities. The Free Wave DGR-115 radios are capable of communicating at 115 kbps up to a range of 20–30 miles, when fed into high gain, directional antennas with a clear line of sight. They differ from most institutional bridges in that they terminate in serial ports that can communicate at 115 kbps, which is generally the highest rated speed of individual computer serial ports. The radios actually can communicate at 180 kbps. The serial port speed is the limiting factor. The price of the radios is $1,250 each, with perhaps $250 worth of antenna and cabling typically needed. 115 kbps is effectively twice the speed of the telephone company's 56 kbps dedicated four copper wire lines. The National Science Foundation Wireless Field Tests for Education have used these radios in several specific ways.[3]

A pair of radios, operating at 115 kbps, connected a media center with 25 Windows 95 workstations at the Monte Vista Middle School with a commercial Internet POP in Alamosa, Colorado, 17 miles away.

A pair of radios, operating between Colorado Center School District's network, which was connected to the Internet by telephone, and a teacher at home a half-mile away in the town, allowed the teacher to access the Internet through her own desktop computer at nights and on weekends, without the use of a home telephone or the need for additional commercial modem lines at the school district.

A pair of radios linked an office in Colorado Springs, which is connected to the Internet by commercial frame relay, and a home office a half-mile away. The office in the home had a website operating continuously on an OS2 machine. Anyone on the Internet was able to access the website over the wireless link, with no incremental telephone company cost to the office or the home user.

Wireless LANs are the next step up in power. They exist in many forms. Separate digital radios, from companies such as Wi-LAN of Calgary, Canada, or Breezecom of Israel, can operate from 5 to 7 miles, depending on line-of-sight conditions and antenna arrays, to link LANS at each end. These radios cost from $1,500 to $3,000, with the antenna and associated equipment costing from $250 to $750 more.

Even more powerful are digital radios that contain TCP/IP and other protocols. They combine the characteristics of wired links plus separate IP routers in one package. Cylink, Persoft, Solectek, Proxim, Karlbridge, and others produce a variety of radios that operate point to point, point to multipoint, relay, or even "channelize" and can support voice channels as well as data channels. They cost from $4,000 to $10,000 each. Solectek has claimed speeds up to 10 megabits per second at one watt of transmitter power, over a line-of-sight distance of 25 miles. This is equal to the claims of most costly microwave systems.

There is already at least one Internet Service Provider (ISP) in California, "Wireless Infonet," that offers only wireless connectivity to the Internet. More companies may be expected to do the same and will likely focus on smaller companies that need something more than a 56bps link to the Internet, but not at local loop T-1 fiber prices.

Domestic Benefits of the Foreign Market

Reed Hundt, the former chairman of the FCC, cited the economic benefits to the United States in the burgeoning number and variety of wireless commercial services being developed, all guaranteed their slice of spectrum by the U.S. government. It will be a very long time, if ever, before world markets will be ready for such advanced commercial services based upon wired-line solutions, since they lack the wired telephone company infrastructure of more advanced nations. There is, therefore, a present market for no-license radios to connect educational, government, and business facilities to the Internet, even in capital cities of the developing world. It is very much in the public interest to encourage such industries to export U.S. products where U.S. telephone-based services have little chance of establishing themselves. It would aid these manufacturing companies in reaching a scale of sales that would help bring down the costs of selling radios in the highly competitive U.S. markets.

The clamor of developing countries to enter the Information Age, by connecting to the Internet in countries with very poor or nonexistent traditional telephone infrastructures, creates a situation that is in the trade interest of the United States. FCC policies that truly serve the public interest might reduce performance and spectrum limits on the production of spread spectrum radios. These policies would expand the ability of U.S. companies to sell large volumes of radios in places where no telephone company can go or wishes to go, perhaps triggering an export surge comparable to that of U.S. personal computers.

Even where distances between towns exceed 25 miles, the ability of well-designed radios to reach 50, 75, or 100 miles without unacceptable losses of bandwidth may solve many connectivity problems in countries to which the United States would like to export and contribute to the U.S. balance of trade. Already, wireless systems, from companies such as Tetherless Access, Ltd., are being deployed in places such as China.

The National Science Foundation supported an instructive effort to put up a test network in Ulaanbaatar, Mongolia. The Mongolian problem was classic. Mongolia could get a 128 kbps satellite Internet link via PacCom, then Sprint Link into one ground station and its associated computers, owned by a small company, DataCom, into a single computer in the center of the capital city. But, the Mongolian telephone company (PTT) did not have the equipment or expertise to extend that link beyond modem dial-up speed to institutions in the city, such as the Mongolian University, the Academy of Science, the National Library, and several government offices.

In two weeks, an NSF-funded team linked seven sites from 1 to 10 kilometers away from the satellite ground station location, using 115 kbps radios from Free Wave. The total cost was roughly $10,000 per site, including all equipment, travel, installation, and training costs. Now that there are experts in Mongolia, further sites might be connected for less than $5,000 per site.

Why should the FCC, or the United States more generally, be interested in the advantages of spread spectrum radios for foreign countries? It is a matter of radio engineering and development costs.

Unless there is a very substantial and growing market for radios so advanced that they can fully reach the potential indicated by radio theory, the development costs will be high. Omnipoint spent over $100 million in engineering costs to develop its new technology digital telephones and achieved order of magnitude improvements over existing telephone technologies. The potential for large sales in foreign, developing markets may act as a big incentive for U.S. companies to undertake further development.

In order to ensure that a large proportion of the U.S. population may use advanced radios without interference, manufacturers must spend the necessary amounts to make the very best possible radios and they must profit from their efforts. Eventually, other countries may be able to design and sell radios as advanced as the American ones, but, at present, this area of radio engineering represents a sector where U.S. technological expertise provides an edge.

The current rules encourage cream skimming—building radios with less than their potential for low interference, selling in a market until interference starts happening, then moving on. There are reports of radios being introduced into the vast, untapped foreign markets and then, as soon as the concentration of radios reaches the point that they interfere with one another, the vendor moves on to another city. With proper design, these congestion problems may be avoided. There must be a powerful incentive for radio companies to do the costly hard engineering in the first place, a research and development cost that will be justified in eventual sales.

New Rules Needed

There are slight signs that growing understanding at the FCC of the possibilities for shared spectrum, in part through demonstrations such as those funded by the National Science Foundation, and the pressures of the 1996 Telecommunications Act may lead to changes in the FCC rules for spread spectrum wireless.

First, the FCC approved what is called the U-NII (Unlicensed-National Information Infrastructure) Bands in the 5.8 GHz area. They permit spread spectrum and other radios operating at 20 megabits per second to be unlicensed across 300 megahertz of bandwidth.

Secondly, the FCC has just ruled that the antenna gain for spread spectrum radios operating in the 2.4 GHz and 5.8 GHz bands may be unlimited (while continuing the one watt limit on the radio itself). Additionally, the FCC has issued a Notice of Inquiry (NOI) addressing the problem of overloaded voice switched-circuit LEC systems, asking for public recommendations on solutions, and even suggesting that wireless may be part of the solution.

This section summarizes the basic principles that the FCC should follow in making rules for such NII Bands—or "community networking" public spectrum.

The rules for the NII Bands should be market-based. No one model will fit all situations. For example, in rural areas, where spectrum interference is lowest, but the need is for greater range, the rules should allow higher effective radiated power, or lower interference-limiting rules, than in dense urban areas, where distances are shorter and congestion greater. Similarly, relaying a message from one radio to another to extend range should not be prohibited when the object is to reach the total population of an area.

The technical rules for the performance of radios in the spectrum—the frequency hopping rules—should minimize the possibility of local interference between like radios. The original rules had a low bar for entry into the Part 15 bands, in order to encourage both experimentation and entry, which led to interference between radios not engineered to a higher spread spectrum standard. Now that processing power is greater and developers have the benefit of more than 10 years of experience with frequency hopping radios, the standard should be raised.

The rules should take into account the rapid growth of processing power and, therefore, potential signal processing power. They should make provisions for changes based upon the greater capabilities. They should stipulate less interference with higher throughput and robustness of operations. It may even be desirable to award licenses to radio manufacturers for a fixed period, such as two, three, or five years, before recertification of the same radios, in order to try constantly to raise acceptable radio performance. This system would create an incentive for designers to build ever better radios to take advantage of the improving capabilities and falling cost of components. Currently radio designs are certified forever and radios with poor performance pollute the spectrum. In other words, technological change must be built into the rulemaking in ways that it has not been before. This rule would impose a level of hardship on some companies, but, if technological progress is the only way to solve the interference problem, then it is in the public interest in affordable access to make this a priority.

The rules should consider complete systems and the way that they will be operated, rather than just discrete radio specifications and separate antenna designs. The design of radios can make a large difference in interference. For example, one manufacturer makes radios that are designed to transmit all the time, rather than just listening before transmitting. This increases interference unnecessarily and puts other more efficient users of spectrum at a disadvantage.

The rules should encourage designers to create radios that search wide spectrum bands, sensing whether there is traffic at the instant, and communicating only where there is none. This would mark a trend away from the historical allocation of discrete and narrower "bands" or channels for operation.

The FCC should approve wattage and antenna gain that would allow communications to at least 15 kilometers in urban and 40 kilometers in rural areas. Further, it should permit antenna designs that make relaying between radios feasible, extending distance to at least 80 kilometers with directional antennas. These developments would help meet the legal mandate of the FCC to find ways to provide universal access to the Internet for all Americans, wherever they live, work, or study, for it might reduce the cost of connecting end-users to the one-time costs for the radios.

Notes

1. Timothy Jason Shepard, "Decentralized Channel Management in Scaleable Multihop Spread-Spectrum Packet Radio Networks" (doctoral thesis, Massachusetts Institute of Technology, MIT/LCS/TR-670, 1995).

2. Gain refers to the ratio of output power to input power.

3. National Science Foundation 1995–1998 Wireless Field Test Reports, <http://wireless.oldcolo.com>.

The Rooftop Community Network: Free, High-Speed Network Access for Communities

David A. Beyer, Mark D. Vestrich, and J. J. Garcia-Luna-Aceves

This chapter describes a new model for delivering high-performance end-user connections to Internet services that may relieve the current dependence on telephone or cable companies to propagate local access infrastructure. The "rooftop community network" uses innovative wireless technology to create fast, robust, community networks, which are constructed entirely by the end-users and are free of monthly operating charges for all traffic over the wireless network. In this way, the rooftop community network turns the telephone and cable companies' infamous "Last Mile Problem" into a "First Mile Opportunity" for end-users and communities.

Users join a rooftop community network by purchasing and installing an "Internet radio" at their home or office. The Internet radio couples a high-speed digital radio with "intelligent" packet-switching software. A rooftop community network is a self-managing web of peer Internet radios, in which each radio serves not only as a user's connection to the network, but also as an automatic repeater to forward other users' traffic, as needed, in its community network. The rooftop community network approach, therefore, extends the distributed, autonomous Internet model to its next revolutionary generation by bringing the switching infrastructure all the way out to the end-users.

Since it conforms to Internet protocol standards, the rooftop community network also enables its users to connect seamlessly to the global Internet. Each user's interconnection costs may be sharply reduced by sharing access to an Internet link among a number of users in the community. Due to its packet-switching technology, a rooftop connection uses network resources only when there is actually data or control information to transmit or receive. Thus, the rooftop network is able to provide continuous connectivity for all users, while still optimizing overall network performance. Continuous connectivity means, for example, that e-mail is delivered instantly without having to "dial up" and that every user may publish information through a website without investing in a dedicated line to the Internet.

This chapter provides a brief introduction to the concept, technology, applications, and policy issues of concern for the rooftop community network.

Your Local Rooftop Network

To join an existing rooftop network, a user must purchase and install an Internet radio and antenna. The Internet radio consists of a high-speed (256 kbps to 10 Mbps or higher) digital radio, which uses radio frequencies that have been set aside by the appropriate regulatory authorities[1] for unlicensed use, and an embedded microcomputer that runs the Internet Radio Operating System (IROS)[2] software. The antenna, which is smaller and simpler than a typical television antenna, is mounted on the user's roof and is connected to the Internet radio with a cable, like that used for cable television. To aid in positioning the antenna, the Internet radio may provide audio or visual indications when it automatically detects radio connectivity with other Internet radios in the rooftop network.

The Internet radio would be connected to the user's computer or to a local computer network in one of three ways: over a simple serial connection to a single computer; over a link to a local area network, such as Ethernet; or over a short-range wireless link to desktop or mobile laptop computers. The third alternative promises to become increasingly attractive as the price of the hardware needed for the Internet radio continues to decline. Lastly, the user would configure the local computers with the proper Internet addresses, in much the same way that they are configured today for dial-up access to the Internet.

Free Networking within the Community

Within a rooftop community network, all the radios automatically participate in forwarding traffic for the network. Anyone with a rooftop connection may send traffic to any other member of the local rooftop community network for free. Unlike a cellular network, there are no base stations that must be installed or maintained (see Figure 1).

Internet Radio Operating System (IROS) software in the radios automatically controls the routing of packets across multiple links between their sources and destinations. This software requires no configuration or intervention by users, beyond that required for connecting a computer to the Internet over a typical dial-up line. In congested networks, IROS software helps to ensure that each user receives a fair share of the network bandwidth by adaptively regulating the slices of time that each radio is used to forward traffic for others. Through the use of pseudo-random radio modulation methods and unique network security keys, the software also helps to guarantee security, so that traffic is protected from eavesdroppers and malicious users. Since the radios use unlicensed spectrum, no licenses are needed to acquire spectrum or to operate the radio. The equipment purchase of Internet radios is the only expense. As a result, for the same reason that kids pay no service charges for communicating around the neighborhood with "walkie-talkies," there are no service charges for communication over a rooftop network.

Since a rooftop community network is based on Internet protocols, members of the network may use the familiar, rapidly growing base of network software applications that have become commonplace on the Internet, including standard Web browsers, e-mail applications, and news readers.

Applications of the free data communication made possible by a rooftop community network include:

• Community education networks. These networks might support a wide range of applications, from multiuser, educational role-playing games among users in homes, local schools, and public libraries to publishing book reports on home websites.

Beyer, Vestrich, and Garcia-Luna-Aceves

Rooftop Networks

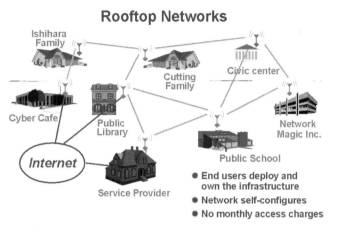

Figure 1

• High-speed "public access networks" or "FreeNets." Rooftop community networks may further stimulate the current explosion of local FreeNets, by eliminating the cost and limitations of the local-loop telephone lines and by making it easy for all members to be publishers of information.

• Business telecommuter networks. Businesses may reduce the cost of having employees work from home by reducing monthly access charges. Firms might also support their communities by sharing the use of their Internet radios to seed neighborhood networks.

• Shared access to community databases. This may include access to local government records, such as the minutes of town assembly meetings or building regulations, or to medical information among multiple hospital sites and their affiliated clinics and doctors' offices.

• Free community e-mail. Probably the simplest, and perhaps most useful, benefit of the rooftop community network is the potential for free e-mail among members of the network, such as between students and teachers or between citizens and local government offices.

The rooftop community network is ideal for disseminating community information for three reasons. First, by limiting the number of Internet radios that may forward a message, broadcasts may be easily limited to the approximate geographic radius appropriate for the message. For a geographic broadcast message, the sender would address the message to the "multicast address group" used to indicate the desired geographic radius. Individual members would choose which of these multicast groups to join and which to ignore. Secondly, messages are delivered immediately, unlike classified ads in printed media, for example. Immediate delivery gives individual members the ability to report emergencies or other events quickly to other people possibly affected. Third, there are no fees or monthly charges for communication within the rooftop network. The members of the network purchase and install the Internet radios that constitute the packet-switching fabric of the network. For communication within the community network, therefore, no commercial service provider is needed.

Examples of community information that may be advantageously distributed over rooftop community networks for free include: neighborhood messaging, such as requests for help in finding a lost pet, and announcements of upcoming garage sales; community events, such as announcements of upcoming fairs and political candidate forums, distributions of the minutes of town government committee minutes and emergency notifications; and commercial events, such as end-of-the-day sale announcements at the local grocery store or solicitations of customers' opinions about which brands to stock. Virtual "subscriptions" may be used to help ensure that users receive such messages only from information types and sources to which they have "subscribed."

Continuous, High-Speed Internet Access at Low Cost

Rooftop community network users will also benefit from high-speed, continuous (24 hours per day), low-cost access to the rest of the Internet. By taking advantage of the typical "bursty" nature of the Internet access needs of individual users (short bursts of high-bandwidth followed by relatively long idle periods), a rooftop community network may effectively share the cost of a single fast link to the Internet among a number of local members. For example, a high-speed, Asymmetric Digital Subscriber Line (ADSL) to an Internet Service Provider (ISP), with a data rate of 6 megabits per second (Mbps) downstream (to the home) and 640 kilobits per second (kbps) upstream might cost $600 for installation and modem equipment, and then $150 per month for phone company and ISP service charges. This cost might be shared by 25 members of a local rooftop community network, with each paying under $500 for their Internet radio and contributing an average of $6 per month for the Internet link. Since only some of these members will be actively using the network at any given time and due to the bursty nature of Internet access, each member will typically benefit from a downstream bandwidth of 1 Mbps or more during each data burst and of 100 kbps or more in upstream bandwidth.

The actual monthly cost charged to each member for accessing the Internet will depend on the way that the Internet connection is provided. The Internet radio that serves as a relay (or "router") into the rest of the Internet is called an AirHead (or, more formally, an Air-to-Internet-Router). The AirHead may be provided by an industrious neighbor, who might charge others $10 or $20 per month for Internet access. An AirHead located at a library or school, however, may provide access to the Internet as a free local community service for nearby rooftop community network members. The Internet radio at the AirHead site is nearly identical to those of other rooftop community network members. The main difference is that the AirHead's Internet radio is connected, usually over a local area network, to a high-speed modem, such as an ADSL modem, that provides the connection to the Internet. In addition, the AirHead member will usually be responsible for a few simple management tasks for the local rooftop network. These tasks may include: assigning Internet addresses, from a list provided by the ISP, to the other members using this AirHead to access the Internet; and granting permission (e.g., by clicking the "Accept" button on an AirHead configuration Web page) to new nodes wishing to join the local rooftop network.

In contrast to dial-up connections, with a rooftop community network a member uses network resources only when actually transmitting or receiving user data. It is possible, therefore, to have continuous connectivity for all users without bogging down the network. Continuous connectivity allows instant delivery of e-mail, rather than requiring the user to solicit it. It also allows a user to become a provider of information by hosting a website on a home computer, without requiring a dedicated phone line.

Starting New Rooftop Networks

Starting a new rooftop network requires only people at two or more nearby sites, such as separate school buildings or the library and local government buildings, who wish to communicate with each other. Others within range of either of the first two sites are able to join the network simply by purchasing and installing their own Internet radios. As new users join the network, the geographical coverage of the network grows, since each new user need only ensure radio connectivity with at least one other existing member of the network.

Improved Internet access will also drive the introduction of new rooftop networks. Two or more neighbors who wish to share a high-speed link to the Internet might start a rooftop network, with one serving as the AirHead, with a wired link to the Internet, and the others sharing the bandwidth and cost of this wired link. Also, ISPs may set up rooftop networks as an untariffed, local-loop bypass method for accessing the Internet. In particular, ISPs in remote or rural areas may start rooftop networks to provide Internet access to those who have no other high-speed options.

Key Enabling Factors

Four trends make rooftop community networks feasible: the exploding, widespread popularity of the Internet has introduced a common, open-architecture set of standards and software tools that facilitates global communication and information sharing; the recent development of integrated, high-performance, digital radios has begun to bring the hardware needed for Internet radios within reach of a wider range of end-users (see the chapter by Hughes); the availability of unlicensed, wireless spectrum allows the ad hoc deployment and propagation of untariffed, high-speed rooftop networks, with no licensing costs or regulatory delays; and the advancement of the Internet Radio Operating System software permits the rapid and easy deployment of self-managing wireless rooftop networks and the seamless integration of these networks with the Internet.

This section discusses these last two trends. Examples of low-cost, digital radio developments include the PRISM digital radio chipset by Harris Semiconductor, the WavePlex spread spectrum radio transceiver by Advanced Microsystems Inc., or the STEL-2000A spread spectrum wireless burst processor by Stanford Telecom Inc.[3]

Availability of Unlicensed Wireless Spectrum

In 1985, the FCC modified its regulations to permit unlicensed digital communications that meet certain "spread spectrum" waveform requirements in the industrial, scientific, and medical (ISM) RF bands of 902–928 megahertz, 2400–2483.5 megahertz, and 5725–5870 megahertz. The regulations limit a transmitter's maximum output power to one watt; the maximum antenna gain at the transmitter is also limited (to six dBi when transmitting at the maximum power). In early 1997, in response to a 1995 petition by Apple Computer, the FCC added 300 megahertz in the 5 GHz band for unlicensed use with similar power regulations (200 megahertz of which is authorized for outdoor use).[4]

Although the lower bands (around 900 megahertz and 2.4 gigahertz) are able to penetrate a limited number of obstructions, such as one or two office walls or a small pocket of trees, the link ranges for all these bands are categorized as "line-of-sight." This means that, to ensure radio connectivity, the transmit and receive antennas should be able to "see" each other over an unobstructed path. The link range will then be limited mainly by the power and specific antennas being used. For these unlicensed bands and power restrictions, typical ranges for individual links will vary from a half-mile to many tens of miles, given unobstructed link paths.

In late 1997, the FCC allocated 5 gigahertz of spectrum for unlicensed use in the "Millimeter Band," from 59 to 64 gigahertz. In this band, link data rates can be extremely high (tens of Mbps). The range of each individual RF link at 60 gigahertz is restricted to a radius of approximately one kilometer, making this band unusable for long-range links, but ideal for neighborhood and local community networks, since interference from transmitters significantly outside this radius will be negligible. Radio components for this band currently are relatively expensive, but their costs are expected to decline to a point within reach of consumers during the next five to ten years.

These revised rules mark significant steps that the FCC has taken toward allowing the introduction of new unlicensed, wireless networks, such as rooftop community networks.

Internet Radio Operating System Software

The Internet Radio Operating System software in a rooftop community network is based on a technology known as Distributed Packet Radio (DPR).[5] DPR protocols manage the self-organization, routing, and security within a rooftop community network. Standard Internet protocols are used to handle the interface between rooftop networks and the Internet.

The underlying concepts of DPR were formulated largely in research and development programs funded by the U.S. Advanced Research Projects Agency (ARPA) from the 1970s through today. These programs were originally given the task of demonstrating a robust, secure, self-organizing, and highly adaptable communication technology by capitalizing on two new technologies: spread spectrum digital radios, which allow for flexible sharing of spectrum and are robust to interference; and packet-switching data communications, which adapt well to network dynamics and allow efficient use of network resources for bursty data traffic. These research and development programs,[6] along with related efforts in the amateur packet radio community,[7] have led to the development of a mature technology that provides the self-managing, secure, efficient, and asynchronous packet-based characteristics needed for the successful introduction of rooftop community networks.

Spurring the Internet Radio Industry

Although digital radios have become more affordable in recent years, no manufacturer has made a radio that combines the low-cost radio components with the processing and memory features required for Internet radios. Current unlicensed digital radios are designed for local area networks and simple point-to-point or point-to-multipoint applications. The real-time processing capability of the radio is typically limited to simple link reliability and channel-access protocols, with the more sophisticated routing and control functions left to wired routers. In order to support rooftop networks, however, the Internet radio must perform all advanced functions, including packet forwarding, distribution of routing information, security protocols, and congestion avoidance. In addition, the link and channel access protocols needed for reliable packet transmission in a peer-to-peer, rooftop network are more sophisticated than those needed for simpler point-to-point or point-to-multipoint networks. Also, for efficient use of the available spectrum, the digital radio hardware must give the embedded Internet Radio Operating System software finer control of radio characteristics, such as transmitting power, frequency, and spreading pattern.

Although current technology would permit the development of Internet radios with a high-volume, end-user price of under $500, the price of current Internet radios, constructed by integrating PC-board-level components from different manufacturers, varies from approximately $2,000 to $6,000. Although this price will allow penetration into certain classes of Internet radio users, such as small businesses or remote areas that lack good-quality wired access,[8] it is too high for the average home consumer. Introduction of an Internet radio with an end-user price of under $1,000 is needed before rooftop community networks may begin to penetrate the home consumer market.

An additional key missing ingredient required to energize the Internet radio industry is the adoption of a standard Internet Radio Application Programming Interface (API) between the radio platform hardware and the embedded Internet Radio Operating System software. A draft Internet Radio API was developed by Beyer, Frivold, Nguyen, and Lewis.[9] The adoption of such an API would permit the independent, uncoupled development of the control software and radio hardware, allowing organizations to focus on their core competencies and providing multiple sources for these two key components of the Internet radio system.

Scaling to Large Rooftop Networks

Although small rooftop community networks are readily envisioned, large rooftop networks serving thousands or tens of thousands of users, or "nodes," in a region are also quite feasible. In designing large-scale rooftop networks, attention must be given to three key technical issues: routing within the rooftop network, routing between the rooftop network and the rest of the Internet, and radio spectrum congestion.

Routing within Large Rooftop Networks

As the number of nodes in a rooftop network increases, so do the size of the network routing tables and the number of control messages needed to update them. As the network control messages become larger and more frequent, however, the bandwidth available for user data traffic is reduced.

One manner of coping with an increasing number of nodes is to assign addresses to the nodes in a way that allows multiple routing table entries to be aggregated into a single entry. For example, fixed nodes may be assigned an address that indicates their geographic neighborhood. Then, a node outside the neighborhood may simply store a single entry in its routing table for all the nodes in an entire neighborhood. Instead of individual entries for each node in the neighborhood, nodes in the neighborhood have entries corresponding to all the other nodes in their neighborhood. A packet destined for a node is first forwarded by Internet radios toward the destination neighborhood. Upon reaching a node within the neighborhood, the packet is then forwarded more precisely toward the destination node. This form of hierarchical routing is an adaptation of the hierarchical routing scheme first proposed by McQuillan, and extended to more efficient routing algorithms by Garcia-Luna-Aceves and Murthy.[10] In order to avoid "traffic congestion" in a large rooftop network, traffic between distant nodes, for example, greater than six to ten hops apart, might be routed to a nearby AirHead for forwarding over the wired Internet to an AirHead near the destination node.

Routing between Large Rooftop Networks and the Internet

Another potential source of network control messages with large routing tables is due to the need to track routing entries for nodes in the global Internet. In order to allow a rooftop network to connect with the rest of the Internet without forcing each node to maintain large routing tables containing the many addresses known for the rest of the Internet, the AirHeads may mask the majority of the routing information from the rest of the rooftop network. The AirHeads may collaborate to decide which one should advertise a route to an aggregate of address ranges in the Internet. Each AirHead may then distribute small routing control messages with a few large Internet address ranges, rather than large routing control messages with numerous small address ranges. A rooftop network node could select an AirHead by choosing the best match between the Internet address it needs to contact and the address ranges advertised.[11] Therefore, AirHeads are the only members of the rooftop network that must handle complex routing tables to connect to the Internet. A similar "route aggregation" strategy by the AirHeads might also help to limit the amount of routing information that the rest of the Internet must learn in order to route traffic to particular nodes within the rooftop network.

Radio Frequency Spectrum Congestion in Large Rooftop Networks

Typically, all the nodes in a rooftop network will share the same overall radio frequency band for their transmissions. As the size of the rooftop network increases, therefore, the traffic demand within this shared band will also rise. This increased demand raises the possibility of reduced network throughput per user. A rooftop network is able to mitigate this concern by using a combination of methods, which may include reducing the power of each transmission to the minimum needed to reach the intended destination; scheduling transmissions within each neighborhood to avoid collisions; and synchronizing the source and destination of each transmission to switch to a waveform that is relatively uncorrelated with transmissions outside the neighborhood. In fact, Shepard has shown that, by combining these methods with advanced "spread spectrum" techniques that allow each radio to receive multiple transmissions simultaneously, rooftop networks are able to remain effective, even as the system scales to millions of nodes concentrated in a metropolitan area.[12]

Regulation and Policy

Three specific areas of regulation and policy may have a significant impact on the rate of deployment of rooftop community networks. Two are local issues: zoning and local taxation. The third issue is federal regulation of radio spectrum.

Local Antenna Regulations

Local zoning might affect antenna installation. The number of new antennas being installed in municipalities for a wide range of applications is exploding. Network operators will install tens of thousands of Personal Communication Service (PCS) antennas in the next few years, institutions will install various microwave antennas of all shapes and sizes, and individuals will install millions of small satellite television receivers. Local governments are attempting to address citizens' concerns about aesthetics, health, and safety stemming from this trend.

For example, the town of Medina, Washington, home of Microsoft CEO Bill Gates, obtained a federal injunction to prevent several wireless network operators from installing PCS antennas on a local commercial building. This location is critical for the provision of radio coverage to PCS users travelling across the bridge that is the main commuter route between downtown Seattle and its eastern suburbs. The issue in this case is neighborhood aesthetics. This affluent residential area would prefer not to have an unsightly "antenna farm" visually polluting its quaint downtown.

In this case, and in similar cases around the country, these PCS antennas are principally being installed and maintained by for-profit network operators. Antennas for rooftop community networks, however, will be installed primarily by individual citizens or local institutions, such as schools and libraries.

Direct Broadcast Satellite (DBS) provides an example that parallels even more closely the antennas for rooftop networks. DBS antennas are deployed by individual citizens, as are rooftop network antennas. There are more than one million DBS antennas in the Unites States alone. Small DBS "dish" antennas, approximately 18 inches in diameter, are installed for personal use by their owners. Even so, some multiunit developments and subdivisions attempt to restrict or control their deployment, on aesthetic grounds. The appearance of a rooftop network antenna is unobtrusive. A typical rooftop antenna might be a dipole antenna—a fiberglass rod, approximately one inch in diameter and three feet long, mounted in a small bracket bolted to a chimney. Another might be a directional antenna, which approximates the general appearance of a common television antenna, but is significantly smaller. Either type would be less obtrusive than either a DBS dish or a regular television antenna.

In order, therefore, to maximize rapid, widespread deployment of rooftop community networks, it is advisable that zoning regulations for rooftop network antennas be no more onerous than those applying to television antennas installed for personal use.

Local Taxation

Some U.S. municipalities are attempting to impose sales taxes on wireless Personal Communication Service or cellular network operators and on Internet Service Providers. Local efforts to tax rooftop community networks would clearly have a chilling effect on their adoption.

The legal and practical basis for such taxation is difficult to identify. Since rooftop community networks would charge no access fees for local traffic, the volume or revenue basis for any sort of traffic-based tax would be elusive. The question of the party to be taxed is also difficult. The owners and operators of the local infrastructure are its users, who receive no cash remuneration for participating in the network. The AirHeads for any community network may consist of both for-profit firms, such as ISPs, and nonprofit institutions, such as schools or libraries. Revenue received from network participants, if any, would most likely be applied to providing access to the rest of the worldwide Internet and, as such, would probably facilitate interstate and international traffic. It is highly questionable whether a local government has the authority to tax this traffic. Nevertheless, the possibility of local taxation will undoubtedly be raised.

The benefits in citizen participation and productivity to be gained from rapid, widespread deployment of rooftop networks in a community far outweigh any possible revenue that might be generated from attempting to tax such networks locally. In fact, municipalities should try to stimulate and possibly even subsidize their growth, rather than inhibit network growth through short-sighted taxes.

Federal Radio Communication Regulations

In the federal realm, the principal regulatory issue affecting the successful deployment of rooftop community networks is the availability of suitable spectrum. Although the core Internet Radio Operating System can run on any digital radio platform, operating at any frequency, users will choose to join a rooftop community network only if the price and performance of Internet radios compare favorably with other alternatives, wired and wireless. Thus, the location and size of the frequency band available for use by rooftop networks will significantly affect their appeal.

The selection of frequency has its biggest impact on the cost of Internet radios. In general, the higher their frequency, the more expensive the components required to build them. The size of the band available affects the maximum data rate, maximum range, and ability to share the spectrum effectively with similar systems in the same area.

Establishing new unlicensed data bands can support multimegabit data rates over ranges of several kilometers for large communities of users. The FCC's ISM-band rulemaking (establishing roughly 250 megahertz of unlicensed spectrum) and its recent rulings establishing an "Unlicensed NII" band (300 megahertz of unlicensed spectrum) and the "Millimeter Band" (5 gigahertz of unlicensed spectrum) represent an excellent start that will prove the viability of the concepts discussed in this chapter. They are insufficient, however, to meet the full potential of delivering low-cost, multimegabit community communication and Internet access to users in both dense, metropolitan areas and sparsely populated, remote regions.

The FCC and Congress have recently adopted spectrum auctions as an easy, albeit temporary, source of revenue. These auctions are typically dominated by large, sometimes foreign corporations or financial operators with access to large pools of Wall Street capital. In the interests of economic diversity, it would seem extremely sensible to resist the temptation of this shortsighted auctioning and instead to expand and further deregulate the segments of spectrum on which small community groups and individual entrepreneurs may experiment. The result will be more innovative, radical ideas with the potential to deliver significant economic and civic benefits to the communities of the 21st century.

Acknowledgments

The writing of this chapter was supported, in part, by Small Business Innovative Research (SBIR) project number DAAB07-96-C-D010, titled "Commercial Distributed Packet Radios and the Wireless Internet." Also, thanks is due to Professor Henry Beyer of Boston University for his helpful review and insightful comments.

Notes

1. In the United States, the Federal Communications Commission (FCC) is the authority responsible for the regulation of all radio frequency bands, including the identification and use of unlicensed bands.

2. Internet Radio Operating System (IROS) is a trademark of Rooftop Communications Corporation.

3. For the "PRISM" radio chipset by Harris Semiconductor, see <http://www.semi.harris.com/comm/prism.htm>; for the WavePlex spread spectrum radio transceiver by Advanced Microsystems Inc. (AMI), see <http://www.amis.com/spd/wireless.html>; and for the STEL-2000A spread spectrum wireless burst processor by Stanford Telecom, see <http://www.stelhq.com/prods_cdma.htm>.

4. Apple Computer Inc., "Petition for Rulemaking for the National Information Infrastructure (NII) Band," *Federal Communications Commission (FCC) Petition RM-8653* (May 1995).

5. D. Beyer, M. Vestrich and B. Nguyen, "Distributed Packet Radio: What Is It? What Good Is It? How Does It Work? How Can It Help You Today?" (Mountain View, CA: Rooftop Communications Corp. Technical Report, 1996).

6. R. E. Kahn, S. A. Gronemeyer et al., "Advances in Packet Radio Technology," *Proceedings of the IEEE* (November 1978); B. Leiner, D. Nielson, and F. Tobagi, "Issues in Packet Radio Network Design," *Proceedings of the IEEE* (January 1987); J. Jubin and J. Tornow, "The DARPA Packet Radio Network Protocols," *Proceedings of the IEEE* (January 1987); D. Beyer, M. Frankel et al., "Packet Radio Network

Research, Development, and Application," *Proceedings of SHAPE Conference on Packet Radio* (Amsterdam: 1989); D. Beyer, "Accomplishments of the DARPA SURAN Program," *Proceedings of MILCOM Conference* (Monterey, California: 1990).

7. P. Karn, "MACA—A New Channel Access Method for Packet Radio," *ARRL/ CRRL Amateur Radio 9th Annual Computer Networking Conference* (London, Ontario: 1990); G. Jones, *Packet Radio: What? Why? How? Articles and Information on General Packet Radio Topics* (Tucson, AZ: Tucson Amateur Packet Radio Corporation, 1995).

8. In fact, at the date of this writing, rooftop networks are being tested at a handful of locations. Some are being used for distributing Internet access to users in underdeveloped areas, while others are being used as a local-loop bypass means to share high-bandwidth Internet access links among a number of users. For instance, a rooftop network with Internet radios at sites including Rooftop Communications Corp. in Mountain View, California, and a local cybercafe ISP (serving as the AirHead) has been Rooftop's sole means of accessing the Internet since November 1997.

9. D. Beyer, T. Frivold et al., "Radio Device API" (Mountain View, CA: Rooftop Communications Corp. Technical Report, 1997). Available at <http:// www.rooftop.com>, click on "Radio Interface."

10. S. Murthy and J. J. Garcia-Luna-Aceves, "Loop-Free Internet Routing Using Hierarchical Routing Trees," *Proceedings of IEEE INFOCOM* (1997); J. McQuillan, "Adaptive Routing Algorithms for Distributed Computer Networks" (Cambridge, MA: BBN Technical Report 2831, 1974).

11. In a large rooftop network, a user's selection of which AirHead to use for traffic to and from the global Internet may also be based on factors such as the number of nodes currently using an AirHead, the number of rooftop network hops an AirHead is from the user's node, and the pricing policy, if any, for using an AirHead.

12. T. J. Shepard, "Decentralized Channel Management in Scaleable Multihop Spread-Spectrum Packet Radio Networks" (doctoral thesis, Massachusetts Institute of Technology, MIT/LCS/TR-670, 1995).

The Use of Existing Electrical Power Lines for High-Speed Communications to the Home

Michael Propp

With impending deregulation, electric utilities are investigating ways in which they might compete through better quality, pricing, and service offerings. The deregulated utility industry will become three separate businesses: power generation, transmission, and local distribution. Local distribution will be very competitive and many utilities will seek to gain a competitive advantage by offering new services in addition to providing electric power and building brand recognition. One approach that utilities may pursue lies in taking advantage of the potential of their vast wiring infrastructures, which are now used to deliver electric power, to serve also as a high-speed communications medium into houses and apartments. Electric utilities might become suppliers of both electric power and high-speed, reliable communications traffic, including Internet access.

The movement toward using power lines for data communications is more advanced in Europe than in the United States. The next section briefly discusses one early project in Spain. The second section describes the potential service offerings by utilities that might make power line communications attractive in the United States. Until recently, the technical obstacles to such communications were formidable. The third section outlines a technical approach that permits fast and reliable communications over power lines, thereby providing potential links for Internet access and other communications services to nearly every residence in the country.

An Early Application of Power Line Communications

Until the late 1980s, it had not been possible to use the alternating current (AC) power line as a communications medium other than for simple applications requiring low-speed communications, such as meter reading or load control. Power line communications connectivity at useful data rates, that is, more than a few hundred bits per second, is confined to the secondary wire of a low voltage distribution transformer, the same wire that distributes electricity to residences. In order to provide communications services over the power line, for example, Internet access, each residence would have to connect to an Internet Service Provider (ISP) through the "first hundred feet" of low voltage electrical wires to a wide area network linked to the ISP. The network topology, therefore, would require a concentrator installed for each distribution transformer, serving to connect communications from each residence supplied by the transformer to a wide area network, via fiber, fixed wireless, or the Public Switched Telephone Network (PSTN), for example.

In the United States, a distribution transformer supplies power to an average of four to six residences. In contrast, each transformer in Europe typically serves several hundred residences. With the concentrator cost distributed over an average of four to six electric meters per distribution transformer in the United States, there is no compelling case for solely providing an automated meter reading service in the United States. In Europe, with several hundred meters per transformer, utilities are moving to adopt automated meter reading over the power line.

One of the first automated meter reading (AMR) projects was Iberdrola's[1] system in northern Spain. The system monitors real-time consumption, time-of-day energy rates, overall system demand, invoice period comparisons, and peak consumption times. The system consists of in-home customer display units, metering devices, and the "electrical power line communications medium," namely the low voltage electrical wire.

The project networked the entire village of Zarauz in the Basque region of northern Spain, using a 19.2 kilobits per second (kbps) throughput power line communications technology. The system was a collaboration between Ikusi[2] of San Sebastian, a Spanish systems integrator and communications equipment manufacturer, and Iberdrola of Bilbao, Spain's largest utility. Ikusi retrofitted approximately 10,000 electric meters for automated meter reading, using the 19.2 kbps power line communications products of Adaptive Networks[3] of Newton, Massachusetts, together with 50 concentrator units located at transformer centers and approximately 1,500 customer display units installed in individual residences. The meters and customer display units were networked through the power line to the concentrators, which, in turn, used telephone lines, radio, and fiber to communicate with a central control and monitoring center.

The customer display unit provided the customer with information on elapsed consumption and cost, the current time-of-day rate, alarms, and messages sent by the utility, and allowed load control for energy management. By bringing information directly to the consumer, the display unit enabled the consumer to make informed decisions about usage of electric power. In buildings where the meters were located in one area, a pulse generator in each meter was connected to a local concentrator, which in turn communicated the data over the power line.

Power Line Communications Applications in the United States

In the United States, the business case for developing power line communications becomes attractive, if the utility introduces services that require higher data rates than those offered by traditional power line communications technologies. With the ability to communicate over the power line at higher data rates, for example, exceeding 100 kbps throughput, meter reading and load control can become one of many services delivered over the existing infrastructure. With deregulation of both the telecommunications and electrical utility industries, utilities have the opportunity to enhance their basic services with a broad array of energy and telecommunications offerings and features. For example, for the four to six homes served by one pole or pad transformer, a utility might offer the following bundle of services:

• Internet access
• Local telephone access

- Automated electric, gas, and water meter reading[4]
- Energy management to minimize electric usage through load shedding and demand side management
- Security services to detect theft, fire, and carbon monoxide or natural gas leaks
- Medical emergency alert
- Tracking of valuable assets located in a residence
- Appliance control and monitoring

As the achievable data rate on the power line increases, the business opportunity becomes more compelling. With the offering of security and medical alert services, the added communications infrastructure costs may then be justified in contrast to solely implementing meter reading. With the power line communications network able to support data rates high enough for Internet access and telephony, an even greater opportunity is presented to the utility for revenue generation.

With the advent of deregulation, utilities may wish to use real-time information from the meter to compete for residential customers. For example, a utility might offer customers a savings plan in which customers may use the communications link to the meter to make informed decisions regarding electricity usage. Security services, further removed from a utility's core business, have already been offered by UtiliCorp United[5] (Kansas City, Missouri), Western Resources Inc.[6] (Topeka, Kansas), and Duke Power[7] (Charlotte, North Carolina). Internet access permits a utility to enter markets even further removed. There may, however, be a convergence among some aggressive utilities and telecommunications service providers. For example, Boston Edison[8] (Boston, Massachusetts) has announced agreements with RCN[9] (Boston, Massachusetts), and Duke Power (Charlotte, North Carolina) and PECO Energy[10] (Philadelphia, Pennsylvania) have invested in personal communication service (PCS) ventures providing digital cellular telephone services. It is, however, a two-way, reliable, secure, high-speed power line communications network, which presents a low cost per network node, that will most easily allow utilities to offer these services.

The Technical Solution

The AC power line has long been recognized as a possible communications medium, although there are significant difficulties, due to data corruption by power line noise and attenuation. In recent years, however, effective solutions to these obstacles have been found.[11] Noise and frequency-dependent signal attenuation are found on almost every power line, resulting in unacceptably high bit error rates. Actual error-free data throughput is always a fraction of the raw data rate.

These obstacles can be overcome through the use of a hierarchical design in which each level of the design is optimized to overcome the inhospitable characteristics of the power line environment. The design hierarchy follows the Open Systems Interconnection reference model of network communications, a model used to govern how networked devices communicate. As in many applications, an abbreviated three-layer version of the model is the appropriate architecture (see Figure 1).

The lower layers of the communications protocol, including the physical layer, a reliable low-level link protocol, and a media access control sublayer, must compensate for the exigencies of the power line. The abbreviated three-layer architecture can be easily implemented using a highly integrated chip set in which one chip controls the physical layer and a second the data link and higher layers (see Figure 2).

The key features that provide immunity from power line attenuation and noise are the use of spread spectrum wideband modulation, fast synchronization, adaptive equalization, error control coding, and power-line-optimized network protocols. A low-cost chip set is able to incorporate these power-line-specific features, permitting electronic product manufacturers easily to incorporate a power line communications capability into devices.

The Power Line Physical Layer

Part 15 of the Federal Communications Commission rules[12] allows power line communication outside the AM frequency band (outside 535 to 1705 KHz). Past efforts to use power lines for commu-

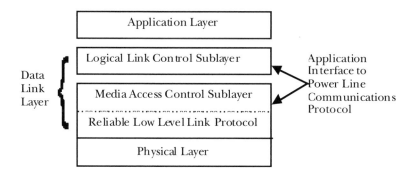

Figure 1 A Power Line Communications Architecture Based on an Abbreviated OSI Three-Layer Reference Model.

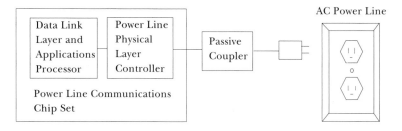

Figure 2 A Highly-Integrated Chip Set Allows a Simple Power Line Communications Implementation.

nication employed modems to modulate a carrier frequency of between 50 and 500 KHz, using frequency shift keying (FSK) or amplitude shift keying (ASK) to achieve digital versions of FM and AM, respectively. These power line communication modems require constant tuning to adjust to changes in signal attenuation and noise when electrical devices are plugged into or unplugged from the electrical network.

In general, spread spectrum systems have better noise immunity than narrowband systems on the power line. Traditional spread spectrum approaches, however, do not solve the difficulty of signal synchronization on the power line impaired by constantly changing noise and frequency-dependent attenuation.

A unique physical layer spread spectrum technology can provide very rapid synchronization. Rapid synchronization is an important component of a fast, practical, and reliable power line communications system enabling a protocol whereby data is transmitted in short frames, that is, continuous sequences of bits. The physical layer also incorporates rapid equalization of the received signal to compensate for the frequency-dependent noise and attenuation.

The Reliable Low Level Link Protocol

Three key features of a data link layer allow large, multinode networks to operate reliably on the power line. First, the link protocol breaks down larger packets of information that are produced by the user's software into smaller power line frames. Small frames are necessary because the longer a transmission, the more likely that it will be corrupted in transit. Second, the link protocol provides rigorous error correction and detection. It attempts to correct errors in the data as a frame is received, then detects uncorrected errors in frames to determine whether the frame should be sent again. Third, the link protocol provides adaptive equalization. Adaptive equalization is necessary because power line noise and attenuation can change every few milliseconds and the receiver will miss transmissions, if it does not adapt quickly by compensating for the changes in the received signal.

The Media Access Control Sublayer

The media access control (MAC) sublayer transfers control of network access using media access control (MAC) algorithms. The MAC algorithms used on dedicated wire are not transferable to the power line. Token passing, however, is uniquely suited to the power line medium.

On the power line, it is difficult to distinguish between noise and signal. Token passing, whereby a token is passed from device to device to transfer control of network access deterministically, ensures only one token holder at any moment in such a noisy environment. A reliable three-way handshake is used to transfer the token between nodes, which ensures an orderly transfer of control without losing the token.

As the location of each node is different, each node hears a particular transmission, subject to different noise and attenuation.

There is thus the possibility that some nodes will miss a transmission that other nodes hear. In token passing, nodes cannot transmit unless they hold the token, so there is no possibility that nodes will start to transmit during another node's transmission.

A Likely Scenario for the Future

Multiple applications of power line communications technology are in use today, including point-of-sale (POS) networks, vending machine monitoring, and an ISO (International Organization for Standardization) standard for communicating aboard refrigerated container ships. These applications illustrate the merits of using the AC power line as a high-speed communications medium, to provide users with easy device portability and to eliminate the cost and inconvenience of installing dedicated wire communications.

Technology to enable power line communications at speeds similar to those of Ethernet will soon become available in products for personal computer (PC) networking within the residence. The advent of this technology will permit utilities to offer high-speed Internet access to and from the residence, without the potentially huge infrastructure investments faced by other service providers. Given the multistage process by which utilities develop new business areas—from establishing a business case to trials to volume use—the initial deployment of high-speed power line communications for the residence will most likely be for communications within the residence, for networking PCs and PC peripherals.

Once such products are in place in residences or small offices, utilities will find that a portion of their customers can receive and transmit power line communications and will be receptive to new service offerings, such as Internet access.[13] As electric utilities begin to explore this avenue for enhanced services, a far greater value will be found in the power line than simply delivering energy.

Notes

1. <http://www.iberdrola.es>.

2. <http://www.ikusi.es>.

3. <http://www.adaptivenetworks.com>.

4. <http://www.iberdrola.es>.

5. Ira Krepchin, "UtiliCorp United, Adaptive Networks Form PLC Team," *Technologies for Energy Management*, Vol. 4, No. 9. See also <http://www.utilicorp.com>.

6. <http://www.wstnres.com>.

7. <http://www.dukepower.com>.

8. Jon Auerbach, and Jerry Ackerman, "In a First, Edison Deal Ties Services," *Boston Globe*, September 30, 1996. See also <http://www.bedison.com>.

9. <http://www.rcn.net>.

10. <http://www.peco.com>.

11. Chris Ladas, "Using AC Power Lines to Network PCs in the SOHO Market," *TIPCIC Proceedings*, December 1996, p. 175; Chris Ladas, "Designing High-Speed Power Line Communication Systems," *Communication Systems Design*, February 1996, pp. 23–32; Chris Ladas, "Power Line Communications: Another Wireless Alternative," *Wireless Design & Development*, November 1995, pp. 17–19; Michael Propp, "Use The AC Power Line as a Wireless Medium," *Microwaves & RF*, May 1995; Frank Goodenough, "Chip Set Puts 100 Kbits/s of Data on Noisy Power Lines," *Electronic Design*, March 18, 1996, pp. 177–184; and Ron Gershon, David Propp, and Michael Propp, "A Token Passing Network for Power Line Communications," *IEEE Transactions on Consumer Electronics*, 37(2):129–134, and the website of Adaptive Networks, Inc., <http://www.adaptivenetworks.com>.

12. Telecommunication, *Code of Federal Regulations*, 47 CFR 15.107.

13. Robert Metcalfe, "Cheap, Reliable, Powerful 'Net Connections May Be as Close as an Electrical Socket," *InfoWorld*, February 10, 1997, p. 44.

Will Satellite Broadband Services Fulfill Their Promise?

Bryan Vu

One of the greatest problems with conventional communications technology is the fact that a very large infrastructure investment is required to build a broadband information network. For example, it is estimated that installing fiber-optic cable throughout the state of California would cost over $15 billion and would take many years. For developing countries, the outlook is even worse. Nations that do not have even the most basic telephone service, electricity, or water cannot hope to build a wireline broadband infrastructure. In the information age, the gap between those who have information and those who do not threatens to grow increasingly wide.

The companies proposing global broadband services believe they have a solution. With a network of satellites covering practically every inch of the globe, these companies claim that they will be able to provide broadband information access to anyone. People will have access to information whether they live in an industrialized or a developing country, a big city or a rural area. A user in the Australian outback will have access to the same information at the same cost as a user in the heart of Manhattan. These are bold claims. But, are they based in fact or will satellites bring less than a total revolution in the way we use information?

This chapter initially discusses the various satellite proposals and assesses their strengths and weaknesses relative to each other. It then addresses potential competition from terrestrial services and possible regulatory obstacles. Next, it describes stratospheric telecommunications services (STS), a technology currently in the early development stages that could eventually compete with satellites. The chapter concludes with some ideas about what shape the broadband satellite market may eventually take.

The Satellite Proposals and Technology

Two basic types of satellite systems have been proposed, geosynchronous earth orbit (GEO) satellites and low earth orbit (LEO) satellites. GEOs orbit in the Clarke belt, approximately 35,000 kilometers (22,000 miles) above the equator. The orbit at this altitude over the equator is the only one in which a satellite can stay over the same area of the earth for an indefinite period of time. At lower altitudes, satellites must orbit at a rate faster than the rotation of the earth in order to maintain their orbits. At altitudes higher than 35,000 kilometers, they must orbit more slowly than the earth's rotation to avoid being flung into space. Each GEO serves one geographic area and can theoretically cover approximately 41 percent of the earth's surface. Companies proposing GEO systems plan to use between three and 15 satellites to deliver worldwide service.[1]

LEOs orbit 20 times closer to the earth, between 700 kilometers (450 miles) and 1,350 kilometers (700 miles) above the earth's surface. Each LEO is moving constantly, covering a particular area for only a few seconds. Thus, a network of many LEO satellites is required to cover the entire world. Two companies have proposed LEO service: Teledesic, backed by McCaw Cellular founder Craig McCaw and Microsoft Chairman Bill Gates, and M-Star, backed by Motorola.[2] M-Star, however, is not aimed at the consumer market. Motorola plans to offer high-bandwidth intercontinental links between network providers.

All wireless communications systems use frequencies within the radio spectrum. Television, radio, cellular and cordless phones, citizens band radios, radar, and radio telescopes are just a few of the users of spectrum. Generally, only one user can use a particular spectrum frequency at one time in the same area. If two users use the same frequency at the same time, interference is created. The Federal Communications Commission (FCC) in the United States and the International Telecommunication Union (ITU) internationally are charged with the task of deciding the spectrum frequencies that will be dedicated to each use.[3]

Along with every other radio communications device, satellites require a piece of the spectrum. At the 1995 World Radiocommunication Conference, the ITU allocated 2.5 gigahertz (GHz) of spectrum for fixed satellite services in the 28 GHz Ka band. Fourteen satellite applicants are vying for pieces of that 2.5 gigahertz. Their requests range from 750 megahertz to the full 2.5 gigahertz, although most applicants are requesting one gigahertz of spectrum.[4]

The Ka band has not been used in the past because such high-frequency transmissions are easily blocked. Buildings, trees, and other solid objects can cause a loss of signal. The Ka band frequencies are unsuitable for use by ground-based systems because they would require a large number of transmitters to be able to avoid all obstacles. Signals from satellites, however, come from directly overhead and are not impeded by buildings and trees.[5]

GEOs: A Proven Technology Limited by the Speed of Light

The primary advantage of GEO satellite systems is that they are a proven technology. Most current communications satellites are GEOs. A limited broadband GEO system, Hughes's DirecPC, is already available.[6]

GEO systems are far less expensive than LEOs. Since a GEO system like Hughes Communications' Spaceway requires only 15 satellites to cover the entire world, Hughes estimates that it can build a global system for only $4 billion. In contrast, Teledesic's 840 satellite constellation is estimated to cost between $9 and $20 billion to build and launch. In addition to having a lower total cost, a GEO system has a far lower up-front capital requirement, since a network of GEOs may be deployed incrementally. Satellites may first be launched over areas of high demand, such as North America or Europe, and revenues from those satellites might then be used to provide capital for additional satellite launches. A smaller number of satellites and launches, together with incremental deployment, might translate into lower costs for consumers.

Another advantage of GEO technology is that the ground stations can be relatively simple because they must only target a fixed point in space. A dish for a broadband GEO would be similar in size and complexity to the direct broadcast satellite (DBS) dishes that are widely available for receiving satellite broadcast services like DirecTV or SkyTV.

The primary and most troubling difficulty for GEO systems is the "latency factor." In order to request information from an Internet server, a signal has to travel 35,000 kilometers to the satellite, then 35,000 kilometers back to the earth. This round-trip takes approximately a quarter of a second. Once the server receives the request, it sends its information on another quarter-second round-trip, for a total latency of a half-second. While the latency factor might be a mere annoyance for routine World Wide Web page downloads, it may be extremely problematic for such interactive uses as videoconferencing. In a video conversation, there will be a half-second delay between the time a speaker finishes and the time he begins to hear and see the other person's response. In a vigorous conversation, it may be difficult to communicate without people on both ends talking over each other. For example, imagine if every time a computer user moved her mouse, it took a half-second for the movement to show up on the screen. It would be very difficult to make fine mouse adjustments. Due to this latency factor, broadband GEO systems are not as attractive for interactive uses as terrestrial and LEO systems.

Another result of the latency problem is that the Transmission Control Protocol/Internet Protocol (TCP/IP), upon which the Internet is based, must either be translated or modified to accommodate the delay. Typically, when a transmission is sent over the Internet, several packets are sent and the receiving computer sends an acknowledgment of their receipt to the originating computer. The originating computer then sends another group of packets. When sending to GEO satellites, the originating computer must wait a half-second between each set of packets. According to a recent NASA study, a TCP/IP system that was designed to transmit data at 155 megabits per second (Mbps) was slowed to near one megabit per second when transmitting through satellites with the half-second delay.[7]

Fortunately, the latency problem may be avoidable. Hughes's DirecPC avoids the problem by using a modified buffer system, in which the originating computer continues to send information without waiting for acknowledgment from the recipient. In addition, the current version of TCP/IP is not well suited for the conventional, wireline, high-bandwidth links that make up the backbone of the Internet and is already in the process of being modified. The modifications may include a solution for the GEOs' TCP/IP transmission problems.[8]

Another potential problem with GEOs is their relatively inefficient reuse of valuable radio spectrum. Since GEOs orbit at 35,000 kilometers, their radio signals cannot stay as tightly focused as those from LEOs or terrestrial wireless systems. Since each radio beam covers a very large area and no beams serving adjacent areas may use the same frequency, a GEO system such as Hughes's Spaceway proposes to reuse the same spectrum frequencies only six times over the continental United States. This will allow Spaceway to provide approximately 2,500 T-1 (1.44 Mbps) connections with 2.5 gigahertz of spectrum. One GEO proposal, by NetSat 28, promises to eliminate the GEOs' spectrum reuse problem with a proprietary technology that the company claims will allow it to provide 500,000 T-1 connections over the continental United States with 1.5 gigahertz of spectrum. This technology, however, is unproven and its practicality is unknown.

LEOs: Ideal, Fiber-Like Transmissions and Egalitarian Deployment—But Are They Feasible?

The great advantage of LEO systems, and the reason that LEOs were proposed as an alternative to GEOs, is that their proximity to the earth's surface gives LEOs a transmission latency similar to that of fiber-optic cable. This means that there is no perceptible delay between the time information is sent and the time it is received. A computer on the ground cannot distinguish between a transmission sent over a LEO network or a wireline fiber network. Instead of transmitting 35,000 kilometers to a GEO satellite, a LEO transmission travels only 700 kilometers, eliminating the latency problem. Videoconferences may be conducted in true real-time and transmission protocols like TCP/IP need no modification.

Another advantage of LEO systems is that they are by nature egalitarian. A low-orbiting satellite covers a small part of the earth's surface at a time, continually changing its service area. LEO satellites move quickly north to south, but their orbits also rotate slowly in a west-to-east direction. Each satellite in the LEO constellation will eventually cover every part of the earth's surface. In order to provide constant service in population centers, the constellation must also provide service to the most deserted areas. A farmer in Ghana would be able to have the same access to the network as an investment banker on Wall Street.

The ability to reuse spectrum more efficiently is another advantage of LEOs. Low-orbit satellites fly much closer to earth, so their beams are more tightly focused when they reach the ground. For example, Teledesic plans to reuse the same one gigahertz of spectrum 20,000 times over the face of the earth and nearly 300 times over the United States, as opposed to only six times over the United States for Hughes's Spaceway.

A third advantage of LEO systems is greater system reliability. In Teledesic's case, each of the 840 satellites will last an average of only ten years. The network will have 42 on-orbit spares already in the sky, however, to replace fallen pieces of the network quickly. Each individual satellite will be less reliable, but the network itself has the ability to compensate more rapidly for failures. A GEO satellite will be far more reliable and last about 15 years, but a single malfunction would interrupt access in the coverage area for the several weeks it would take to launch a new satellite.[9]

The greatest obstacle to launching a broadband LEO system is financial. Teledesic optimistically estimates that it will cost about $9 billion to launch 840 satellites and to begin service. Some analysts have estimated that the cost might realistically be two or three times that amount. Also, since a LEO system is practically impossible to deploy incrementally, the entire investment must be made before any revenues are earned.

Another problem for Teledesic is the large number of satellites that must be launched. When Motorola proposed launching 66 satellites for its Iridium worldwide mobile telephone service, the number was considered to be extremely high. Teledesic is now proposing to launch nearly 15 times that number. At this time, there are approximately 200 satellites in orbit. Teledesic is proposing to launch 840 satellites in one year, several times more than the entire rest of the world has launched in the 30 years since the advent of the communications satellite. There may be complex issues involved in mass-producing a large number of satellites. In addition, questions remain about whether enough launch vehicles exist in the entire world to launch 840 satellites. Teledesic and Lockheed Martin believe it is possible. They claim that, since Teledesic's satellites are small and will only be launched to a low orbit, several can be placed into orbit by a single vehicle. This strategy would reduce costs and require fewer launches and launch vehicles.[10]

Any broadband communications system must be economical for the consumer if it is to be widely adopted. For Teledesic, another possible problem is the high cost of ground stations. A Teledesic ground station must track quickly moving satellites and manage handoffs from one satellite to another as different satellites move over the service area. Typically, this would mean that a ground station would have to be composed of two dishes. The dishes would need to physically rotate to point directly at each satellite as it moved through the service area. As one dish tracked a satellite leaving the service area to the south, another satellite would be entering from the north, and its signal would need to be immediately acquired by a second dish. This solution would be extremely expensive. Since each customer must purchase its own ground station, this cost may make the system impractical for the consumer market, especially in developing countries. Teledesic is currently attempting to solve this problem by using a phased array dish that activates different areas on a single, fixed dish as satellites move overhead. Phased arrays are currently far too expensive for the average consumer, but Teledesic is planning to find ways to lower their cost to approximately $1,000 by the time the rest of the system is ready in 2003.

How Will the Competition between GEOs and LEOs Play Out?

As long as radio waves travel at the speed of light, GEO systems will always have a transmission delay. The lag is acceptable for some applications, such as large file downloads and Internet browsing, and perhaps even for videoconferencing, although heated conversations might be awkward. Ultimately, the applications and consumer preferences of the future will determine the acceptability of a half-second delay. It is almost certain, however, that at least one two-way broadband GEO system will be launched in the next few years. Once the FCC and the ITU give regulatory approval, GEOs will be launched. Hughes plans to begin Spaceway service to the United States in 2002. For GEOs, the technological and financial obstacles have already been cleared.

Compared to GEOs, LEOs offer more attractive, low-latency communications, but much technological and financial uncertainty still remains. A project as technologically ambitious as Teledesic's network must surmount many obstacles. The cost and feasibility of a large number of satellite launches and the possibility of lowering the cost of phased array receivers are outstanding questions. Teledesic must also raise a huge amount of capital. Although it does have well-financed backers in Craig McCaw and Bill Gates, the company will need many more international partners. Unlike GEOs, whose technology and financing exists, it is not certain that Teledesic will be able to begin service in 2003, as projected.

Terrestrial Competition

Satellites will compete with terrestrial technologies for both start-up capital and customers. Traditional wireline fiber-optic cable is the most obvious competitor. Although fiber networks, with an estimated average cost of $1,500 per home, are extremely expensive, they offer bandwidth of up to one gigabit per second with current state-of-the-art equipment.[11] Other wireline technologies include Asymmetric Digital Subscriber Line (ADSL), which can transmit up to six megabits per second to the home and 640 kilobits from the home over standard twisted-pair copper telephone lines using special modems. ADSL is cheaper than fiber at approximately $1,300 per home passed, but it is still very expensive and may be adversely affected by phone line interference.[12]

Cable modems, which use the coaxial cable that currently delivers cable television to many homes, have met with limited success.

Table 1 A Comparison of the Leading GEO and LEO Systems

	Hughes's Spaceway (GEO)	Teledesic (LEO)
Estimated Cost	$4 Billion	$9–20 Billion
End-user Data Rate	1.5–6 Mbps	16 kbps–2 Mbps
Terminal Cost	Under $1,000	$1,000–$8,000
Number of Satellites	15	840
Capacity*	20,000 T-1 connections	20,000 T-1 connections
Spectrum Request	2.5 GHz	1 GHz

*Capacity refers to the number of simultaneous connections. Users are not constantly connected, so the actual number of subscribers may be several times the capacity.

Source: George Gilder, "Telecosm Ethersphere," *Forbes*, October 10, 1994.

The coaxial cable can carry data at rates of between 1.5 and 10 megabits per second but is generally capable of only one-way transmission. In order to provide Internet access, cable operators must make expensive upgrades to their systems, at an average cost of $550 per home, and the consumer must also invest $500 in a cable modem in order to receive the signal.

Terrestrial wireless technologies, such as local multipoint distribution service (LMDS) or multipoint multichannel distribution service (MMDS), are also potential competitors. Wireless systems can cover large areas much more cost-effectively than wireline systems, but since they use high frequencies similar to those used by satellites, they can only connect with receivers that are directly in the line of sight of the transmitter, and blocking by trees and buildings may cause problems.[13]

An important comparison between satellite and terrestrial technologies is cost. Satellite services are more cost-effective per customer than terrestrial technologies in sparsely populated areas and areas with difficult geographic topology. It is extremely expensive to lay fiber or to install a wireless transmitter in areas where only a few customers would be served, but a satellite system serves rural areas at the same cost as urban areas. Conversely, terrestrial systems may be deployed relatively cheaply in populated areas.

While the $3–20 billion capital investment for a global satellite system is large, it is small compared to the hundreds of billions of dollars that it would cost to deploy terrestrial technologies in the United States alone. It has been estimated that the cost to bring fiber-optic lines into every American home would be approximately $300 billion. Since terrestrial technologies are deployed incrementally, their up-front costs are far lower than those of satellites. Even the least capital-intensive GEO satellite projects must spend several hundred million dollars before signing up their first customer.

As a result of spectrum scarcity, satellites cannot provide enough bandwidth to serve all users. Spaceway plans to offer bandwidth for only 2,500 T-1 connections throughout the United States.[14] Teledesic plans to offer 18,000 voice or 18 T-1 connections within service areas of 53 square kilometers each.[15] It seems clear that a city like Washington or New York would require bandwidth many times that which can be provided by a satellite system. (If NetSat 28's proprietary technology does allow it to provide 500,000 T-1 connections in the continental United States as promised, satellites might prove feasible in urban areas.)

Another important issue is spectrum allocation. Currently, terrestrial wireless services must pay for spectrum at FCC auctions. Satellite systems are allocated spectrum by the FCC and the ITU according to the financial viability of the firms requesting the spectrum. Since satellite companies do not have to pay for their spectrum, they gain an advantage. They cannot reuse spectrum, however, nearly as often or as efficiently as terrestrial systems. Spectrum is cheaper for satellites, but satellites have much more limited bandwidth. This scheme of spectrum allocation also works to make satellites more cost-effective than terrestrial wireless technologies in remote areas and less feasible in urban ones. Terrestrial wireline services like fiber, ADSL, or cable modems do not require spectrum.

In the near future, terrestrial services will most likely be cheaper to use in densely subscribed areas. Barring a major technological breakthrough, satellites will not have the bandwidth to serve large cities, even if they could provide service cheaply. But in rural areas or in developing countries that lack terrestrial infrastructure, satellites may be an effective means of delivering information.

Another Possible Competitor: Stratospheric
Telecommunications Service

The Stratospheric Telecommunication Service (STS), proposed by
Sky Station International, Inc., is neither a satellite nor a terrestrial
service but may eventually become a competitive alternative for
local access. An STS is a floating communications platform sus-
pended 20 miles above the earth by helium balloons, higher than
any conventional aircraft, but lower than any satellite. Sky Station
proposes to launch 250 STS platforms, covering every major city
and 80 percent of the earth's population. According to Sky Station,
stratospheric platforms are far cheaper than satellites because they
have very low launch costs and are not as technically complicated.
    A second advantage of an STS system is its ability to reuse
spectrum. Since STS platforms are 20 times closer to the earth than
LEOs and 400 times closer than GEOs, they can use spectrum many
times more efficiently. In light of this spectrum efficiency and lower
cost per platform, Sky Station estimates that its consumer costs will
be approximately ten cents per minute for a 64 kbps channel, with
ground stations that will be cheaper than those for either GEO or
LEO systems. Spectrum efficiency would also give STS platforms
enough bandwidth to serve large cities. A third advantage is that
there would be no latency problem.[16]
    In order to begin operation, STS systems must satisfy regulators
and prove their technology. The first question is one of safety.
Unlike satellites, 37-ton STS systems do not burn up before falling
to earth and, since they would be hovering over large cities, a fallen
platform could cause a great deal of damage. The Federal Aviation
Administration has, however, given Sky Station preliminary approval for STS systems because a number of backup safety devices
have been developed. The primary safety device is a multiple-
balloon design, in which an STS platform's primary balloon would
actually be composed of a number of smaller balloons enclosed by
a large outer balloon. If one of the balloons were to puncture, the
platform would still have enough buoyancy remaining in its other
balloons to be floated down slowly and landed safely.
    Another difficulty arises from spectrum scarcity. The more desir-
able lower frequencies have already been allocated for other uses,

so STS systems will use even higher frequencies than satellites, in the 47 GHz range. At such high frequencies, tree leaves, windows, and even heavy rainstorms could block an STS signal. Supporters of the STS systems claim that they will have enough bandwidth and low enough costs that they could be deployed in both urban and rural areas and in both rich and poor countries. As with satellites, however, STS systems have many issues that have yet to be addressed.

Regulatory Obstacles Facing LEOs and GEOs

In order to deploy their systems, satellite companies must persuade the governments of the world to allocate the spectrum that they need. The 14 satellite applicants in the 28 GHz Ka band are working to lobby the FCC, the ITU, and other governmental bodies for spectrum. Since they cannot be deployed incrementally, LEO systems must have approval from a large number of countries worldwide before operation is feasible. Developers of GEO systems may lobby governments in particular regions of the world and begin service to those areas first. This section reviews several of the more prominent arguments for regulation that may slow or prevent the launch of satellite systems.

European governments may be opposed to a perceived American monopoly of telecommunications infrastructure in space, a concern that has been voiced primarily as a response to Teledesic's proposal. Due to the tremendous barriers to entry associated with a system as capital-intensive and technologically sophisticated as a global LEO system, it is unlikely that a competitor would emerge. European governments are hesitant, therefore, to give spectrum rights for their countries to an American company.

A concern advanced by developing countries is that foreign-owned satellite networks would reduce use of their government-owned telecommunications monopolies, thereby reducing government revenue. Developing countries are generally positive, however, about an infrastructure development that might help them compete with the information-rich countries of the industrial world.

One of the most attractive features of satellites, their ability to transcend national boundaries, is seen by some leaders as a possible threat to national sovereignty. An additional concern is that countries subject to economic sanctions would also receive service. Satellite companies are promising that their signals will be controlled to avoid areas that do not wish or are not permitted to receive service.

In the international negotiations conducted so far, satellite companies' prospects seem good. The ITU has already allocated 2.5 gigahertz internationally for fixed satellite services like broadband LEOs and GEOs. Also, effective lobbying by Teledesic and the U.S. government at the ITU's 1995 World Radiocommunication Conference (WRC) resulted in 0.8 gigahertz being allocated for LEO fixed satellite services worldwide. The 1997 WRC allocated an additional 0.2 gigahertz.[17]

Possible Scenarios

It is clear that uncertainties surround both satellites and STS systems. A goal as ambitious as providing worldwide broadband communications will be inherently difficult to achieve. For satellites, many issues remain about deployment dates, cost, and technological feasibility. It remains to be seen how many of the 14 applicants for spectrum in the Ka band will actually deploy a system. Below are some possible scenarios.

Both GEO and LEO satellites prove feasible, but at a higher cost than terrestrial technologies. This seems the most likely scenario, with cheaper terrestrial technologies being implemented in cities and populated areas and satellite systems serving rural areas and developing countries. Global GEO systems will probably be launched first, with LEOs arriving several years later. LEO competition will lower GEO prices and offer delay-free data transfers. It is doubtful that all 14 companies applying for spectrum in the 28 GHz band will actually launch systems. Several companies may not be granted spectrum, and the smaller of the companies that are granted spectrum may sell it to larger competitors. If satellites are deployed successfully, access to broadband technology may become almost universal, although it will still be cheaper in urban areas and developed countries.

GEO systems dominate the satellite market. LEO systems do not become available due to technical or other reasons. As a result of the limited bandwidth and inherent delay problem of GEO satellites, terrestrial technologies will be the primary method of data access. Rural areas and developing countries will only be able to get access from GEOs with delayed transmissions. Broadband access will remain a limited resource, available only to the rich for the foreseeable future.

LEO systems become available with costs as low as those for terrestrial technologies. The vision of an egalitarian information resource will be realized. Everyone, no matter where they are in the world, will have access to information at the same costs. Due to spectrum and bandwidth limitations, residents in urban areas will probably get their access from terrestrial systems, but not at a significant discount from satellite systems. Access will be nearly universal.

STS systems become available at their estimated costs, at the estimated time, and with the expected bandwidth capability. STS systems could become the broadband access method of choice for urban and rural areas and developed and developing countries, if they can be deployed as cheaply as their proponents claim.

Satellite and STS systems face a daunting number of technical, financial and competitive challenges. If the companies proposing satellite and STS systems are able to succeed in turning their visions into reality, however, they might, in addition to enabling such uses as videoconferencing and telemedicine, make possible many applications that have not yet even been conceived. When the telephone was invented in the 1870s, its inventors had no idea how much it would transform the world. There were no predictions that the telephone would enable the creation of fax machines, voice mail, cellular phones or internets. Similarly, high-speed, ubiquitous, global data access has the potential to change communications in ways that cannot be imagined today. The next few years will be crucial to determining whether or not that potential will be fulfilled.

Acknowledgments

Thanks to Kim Malone and Joe Heaps for their guidance. Also thanks to Larry Williams of Teledesic, Jim Justiss of Hughes Communications, Chris Patusky of Sky Station International, John Williams of the Federal Communications Commission, and the many others who provided background material for this project.

Notes

1. Federal Communications Commission Summary of Ka-Band Applications (1996). Companies planning to bring GEO service in some capacity include: Spaceway (Hughes Communications), Millenium (Comm, Inc.), Echostar, GE*Star, KaStar, Astrolink (Lockheed Martin), Cyberstar (Loral), Morning Star, Net Sat 28, Orion, and PanAmSat.

2. "Satellite Industry Overview," Salomon Brothers, January 24, 1996.

3. Dale N. Hatfield, "The Technology Basis for Wireless Communications," *The Emerging World of Wireless Communications* (Institute for Information Studies, 1996).

4. Federal Communications Commission Rulemaking to Establish Rules and Policies for Local Multipoint Distribution Services and Fixed Satellite Services, CC Docket No. 92-297, July 28, 1995.

5. Hatfield, "The Technology Basis for Wireless Communications."

6. DirecPC currently offers 400 kbps Internet access. Satellite communication is used only for communications going to the end user, while a regular phone line is used for outgoing data.

7. Jube Shriver, "Satellite Firms Dealt Blow on Internet Plans," *Los Angeles Times,* October 3, 1996, p. D1.

8. Dante DeLucia and Youngguang Zhang, "Global Internet over Satellite: Issues, Pitfalls and Potential," Hughes Research Laboratories, Malibu, CA, October 25, 1996.

9. Application of Teledesic Corporation to United States Federal Communications Commission for a Low Earth Orbit (LEO) Satellite System, March 21, 1994.

10. "Teledesic Launch Campaign Capacity and Rates," Martin Marietta Launch Systems Division, September 1994.

11 Jeff Hecht, *Understanding Fiber Optics.* (Indianapolis, IN: SAMS Publishing, 1993).

12. "High-Speed Internet Access Technologies and Markets," IGI Consulting, Boston, MA, 1996.

13. David Mallof, President, WebCel Communications, presentation at the Harvard Information Infrastructure Project Conference on "The First 100 Feet," October 1996.

14. "The Spaceway System," Hughes Communications, Malibu, CA, 1996.

15. Application of Teledesic Corporation to United States Federal Communications Commission for a Low Earth Orbit (LEO) Satellite System, March 21, 1994.

16. Application of Sky Station International, Inc., March 20, 1996.

17. Jorn Christensen, "WRC-95: Results Related to Satellite Communications," *Via Satellite* (February 1996).

Opportunities and Challenges for Nontraditional Providers

A City Guide: Developing, Using, and Regulating Regional Telecommunications Networks under the Telecommunications Act of 1996

Andrea L. Johnson

American cities are pursuing a variety of initiatives to ensure the provision of advanced communications services to their citizenry. Traditionally, cities have had three roles related to the provision of telecommunications services: as regulators of telecommunications under their local franchise authority; as providers of telecommunications services, through internal government networks called virtual private networks (VPNs),[1] or through municipally owned utilities; and as users of telecommunications services. With the passage of the Telecommunications Act of 1996, these roles are changing. The Act restricts the ability of cities to regulate telecommunications providers. In addition, the economics of building new telecommunications infrastructure makes it impractical for most cities to accept the challenge alone. As a result, many cities have considered strategic partnerships to achieve economies of scale, to become public providers of regional telecommunications services, or to aggregate cities' needs to get favorable rates from existing providers, such as the telephone or cable companies. This chapter will focus on city efforts as developers, regulators, and users of regional telecommunication networks (RTNs)[2] under the Telecommunications Act of 1996. It will highlight the examples of several California cities.

As dealt with in this chapter, municipal RTNs are region-wide, open, switched digital broadband networks that are owned or controlled by cities, and that can provide voice, data, cable, and videoconferencing services at a reasonable cost to homes, businesses, and public buildings. RTNs may compete with existing and new providers for telecommunications services: local exchange companies (LECs), such as Ameritech or Pacific Bell; long-distance carriers (IXCs), such as AT&T, Sprint or MCI; or competitive access providers (CAPs), such as LCI, which lease access and resell services to consumers. Cities, like all providers of telecommunications services, are regulated by the federal Telecommunications Act of 1996.

Cities have an interest in developing RTNs to protect public safety and welfare; to enhance internal operations and the administration of services to the public; to foster economic development; and to ensure universal access to telecommunications services at affordable prices. In addition, many cities have traditionally relied upon revenue generated from telecommunications providers through franchise fees, compensation for use of public rights-of-way, and utility user taxes imposed on utilities to pay for public works, improvements, and other public-sponsored services. The Act threatens to eliminate these sources of revenue. In addition, cities also rely upon revenue from sales and gasoline taxes, and incidental transactional costs such as tolls and messenger services, which may be reduced as electronic transactions increase. While innovations create efficiencies for both the government and the public, they also mean that governments must seek alternate sources of revenue to continue to provide the same public services.

Many cities saw passage of the Telecommunications Act as making it easier to develop RTNs, so that residents and businesses might have equal and universal access to new services at affordable prices. Instead, the economics of developing the infrastructure, the financial constraints of cities, the lack of technical standards and interest from existing providers in partnering with cities, coupled with the uncertainty of market demand for new services, make developing RTNs impractical for most cities. The only exceptions are cities that already have municipally owned utilities, which may be expanded and upgraded in stages, as demand increases.

The first section of this chapter examines the manner in which the Telecommunications Act fosters competition and delegates authority to regulate telecommunications. The second section discusses critical issues that cities must resolve as providers of RTNs. The third section explores the ways that cities may leverage their role as users of communications services to obtain favorable rates and to ensure universal access. The fourth section examines the impact of the Act on cities as regulators of RTNs and suggests alternate revenue sources for cities.

Implementation of the Telecommunications Act

The Telecommunications Act of 1996 provides a general framework for achieving competition in interstate and intrastate telecommunications services, and delineates the delegation of authority at the federal, state, and local levels. The Act permits cities as providers of RTNs to compete for telecommunications services and allows users to negotiate favorable terms with telecommunications providers. Implementation of the act has been delegated to the Federal Communications Commission (FCC) and state public utility commissions (PUCs), although the scope of each agency's authority remains unsettled, and has been the subject of litigation.

Fostering Competition

The Telecommunications Act is intended to foster competition for all telecommunications services by lifting restrictions imposed on telephone companies and cable companies and by creating a new class of provider called "telecommunications carriers" that either construct their own facilities or resell services of other providers.[3] Telephone and cable companies must also lease access to their networks and utility poles to resellers on a nondiscriminatory basis.[4] Rates and terms for access and interconnection must be "just and reasonable." State PUCs have the authority to arbitrate complaints among providers where discrimination is found and the FCC has authority to resolve jurisdictional issues.

The franchise authority of cities to regulate telecommunications carriers is restricted, but cities are allowed to receive compensation for use of public rights-of-way. This compensation is intended to cover the cost of interference with public streets and of digging up and repairing the streets.

The Telecommunications Act also preempts the states and cities from promulgating any rules or taking any unreasonable actions that create market barriers to entry in interstate or intrastate markets.[5] The interpretation of this section is a major point of debate because it will define the limits within which a city may operate. The FCC has authority under the Telecommunications Act to preempt city authority where it is found to create entry barriers in violation of the Act or state PUC rules.

City Options As Providers of RTNs

Approximately 100 municipal RTN programs are in various stages of development in the United States, most of which preceded passage of the Telecommunications Act. These programs reflect a "bottom-up" approach to infrastructure development, whereby cities or towns build the infrastructure. In California, for example, cities' needs are too diverse to be addressed effectively by a state-wide initiative. California cities are undertaking infrastructure development on their own or in partnership with other cities or counties. Cities, such as Anaheim, Santa Clara, San Jose, and Palo Alto, are upgrading existing municipally owned utilities for residential telecommunications services. The City of Anaheim has a municipally run electric utility and internal telephone system. The city has chosen to utilize 50 miles of its existing fiber optic infrastructure in building a "universal telecommunications system" to connect the city's businesses, schools, residences, and government buildings. This system will compete with existing providers.[6]

Municipal RTNs

There are two ways that a municipal RTN may provide telecommunications services to the public. The first is as a facilities-based carrier. The city would own, control, and have the responsibility for the operation and maintenance of its own network.[7] The second is as a reseller. In this case, rather than construct a facility, the city would lease or purchase access and equipment from a provider and resell it to consumers, which may be municipal agencies.

As a facilities-based carrier, a municipal RTN might sell or lease its facilities, lines, or conduits to any person. A municipal RTN would be required, in the same manner as other telecommunications carriers, to become certified and to file tariffs with the state

PUC for telecommunications services. In addition, a facilities-based carrier must make its services available for resale to other telecommunications carriers on a nondiscriminatory basis. Redlining or selectively providing service is prohibited and subject to strong action by the FCC.

Cities may also resell the services of LECs and long distance providers. As a reseller, a city would not be limited to providing services within the city or the surrounding region, but might apply for statewide authority. As with a facilities-based provider, a municipal reseller would not be able to discriminate or select the type of customer to service and would have to file for certification with the state.

Many municipally owned public utilities that provide electricity and telecommunications services are set up as cooperatives and are, therefore, exempt from state regulation governing utilities, rights-of-way, or pole attachments.[8] As a result, these municipal utilities may enjoy the same rights as private providers in imposing access fees to their facilities, even though cities are normally restricted, as regulators under the Telecommunications Act, in their ability to impose fees on telecommunication providers. Municipal utilities would also have broad discretion in their service offerings and operations and might more readily compete with other private telecommunications providers, if they are structured as cooperatives.

While the Telecommunications Act generally permits LEC providers to earn a reasonable profit for interconnection, a charter city, such as San Diego, California, is generally precluded from making a profit on business enterprises.[9] In such cities, municipal utilities are only permitted to charge rates that will allow them to be self-supporting.

Critical Issues in Developing RTNs

Cities must resolve three critical issues in the development of RTNs. First, they must decide on the network architecture. There are a variety of network configurations that may be employed, such as the hybrid fiber-coax systems used by cable companies and the hybrid fiber-copper or twisted-pair systems employed by telephone and electric companies.[10] Each system has advantages and limitations. Moreover, today's state-of-the-art technology may well be outdated by the time the network is completed. While some cities are taking a gamble and selecting one standard over another, most cities are ill equipped to gamble on any one technology, perhaps because their hybrid systems currently utilize multiple architectures.[11]

Providers face the same dilemma in terms of technology, which means that in the short term, cities should not expect providers to build a seamless, ubiquitous network. Interconnectivity among providers is impractical because telephone companies, cable companies, and CAPs employ different, competing, and often incompatible technologies to provide the same services. Consequently, it may be more prudent for governments to maintain existing relations with multiple providers and upgrade hybrid systems until the industry becomes more mature.

The LECs and cable companies seem to have little interest in working with cities to build RTNs. Existing providers are already making the capital investment to compete for existing and new telecommunications markets. It is generally private industry, not local government, that has the financial and technical means to develop the necessary infrastructure. As a result, firms see little value in having the government as an equity partner. They may also see the government as a competitive threat in its role as an RTN provider. Providers are diversifying into other areas, but are aggressively protecting existing markets. It is also unclear whether the market in most metropolitan areas is able to support competition by telephone and cable companies, CAPs, and local governments.

Secondly, since cities must generally form partnerships to create RTNs, they must decide upon the nature and extent of their equity participation and whether they wish to compete with existing private providers, such as the LECs, for consumer and business markets. Most cities are ill equipped to handle the marketing and administration required to compete for such markets, nor do they have the technical expertise to maintain the network systems.

Equity participation allows a city to ensure openness and universal access and also provides an ongoing revenue stream. The problem is that the level of equity participation that may be negotiated by a city often depends upon a city's contribution of money or in-kind services or its willingness to grant tax relief or other concessions or to be "at risk" for the debt obligations of the project. Cities typically have public facilities, property, and rights-of-way, including utility poles, that may be contributed, as well as the authority to waive fees and taxes as incentives for equity participation.

The strategic partners of both Anaheim and Austin are CAPs. CAPs and some long-distance carriers seem willing to give cities equity interests, in order to gain access to new markets and to ensure a substantial customer base to support their investment. Unfortunately, their proposals often include the requirement that cities be liable for debt financing obligations, a risk that many cities are unwilling to accept. The advantages of equity participation must be balanced with the associated risks of debt obligation. In Austin, Texas, for example, regulators concluded that voters would not approve tax-free municipal bond financing for the construction of an RTN, so they had to accept a smaller equity stake.[12]

Proposals that include equity participation seem less likely to come from providers that are already established in a particular area. In San Diego, for example, neither of the existing providers proposed equity participation for the city, even though the city had stated its desire for such participation in its request for proposals.

Finally, cities must decide how they will finance the project. Building an RTN from the bottom up without a partner is often fiscally impossible. The capital costs are significant and there is great uncertainty about the applications and services that are needed to generate the revenue to support such a network. There are also recurring management and administrative costs, which often cannot be met from revenue sources. Most cities lack the in-house technical support to manage and maintain their networks, so those services must be contracted to outside vendors. Providers with existing networks, therefore, have a competitive advantage in upgrading their networks because they achieve economies of scale by consolidating operations and restructuring their pricing schedules, so that new upgrades are offset against current revenue.

Financing plans in which a city is not at risk may also be highly speculative. For example, Anaheim is using project financing to develop its network at a cost of $50–60 million. Financing for the second phase will be contingent upon revenue generated from the completed first phase. Phase one will connect commercial, industrial, and government buildings with fiber-optic cable. Phase two will extend the telecommunications system to residential areas. If there is insufficient revenue from phase one, phase two may not be built.

Sometimes the financial risks cause cities to modify or abandon plans. The cities of San Diego and Seattle, Washington, for example, abandoned plans to build an RTN or expand their existing public utility after passage of the Telecommunications Act, citing financing risks and technology concerns. Instead, both cities are upgrading their VPNs.

Cities As Users of RTNs

As users of RTNs, cities have two primary goals: to ensure favorable rates for city government services and to ensure that residents have universal access to telecommunications services at affordable prices. In some ways, these two goals conflict. The need for reasonable access and interconnection rates from providers must be reconciled with universal access, which providers must subsidize. While universal service will likely be achieved through federal and state regulation, it is also possible for cities to sometimes leverage their role as users to obtain favorable rates for their residents.

Leveraging City User Needs for Favorable Rates

Cities that choose not to build RTNs may instead opt to upgrade their existing VPNs and rely upon competition among private providers to address concerns of universal service and fair rates. For example, Sunnyvale, California, which chose not to compete as a gateway with private providers, has formed a strategic partnership with nine other Santa Clara counties to aggregate their purchasing power with existing providers.[13] This partnership is negotiating with Pacific Bell to rebuild its county infrastructure to allow video and data services, in addition to voice. The city of Sunnyvale also maintains VPNs to meet internal needs.

The city of San Diego has joined with San Diego County to develop a VPN to serve their internal and regional needs. The network will be composed of San Diego's existing networks, which serve the city government, city and county libraries and several regional courts within the San Diego area.[14] This network includes a private, switched, integrated PBX telephone network and a broadband data network linking local area networks. It is proposed that this network will be upgraded and expanded with fiber nodes.

Where cities or regions have decided to band together, they have been able to negotiate favorable terms, such as "postalized" rates for access.[15] For example, the Department of Administrative Services in Ohio obtained from its existing carriers, Ameritech and LCI, favorable postalized rates for government and institutional users. While such rates do not permit commercial use or resale use, providers do seem amenable to offering discounts to large customers.

Universal Service

The challenge for proponents of universal access is to design a market system that will drive subsidy levels down over time. Traditionally, "universal service" has meant access to basic voice telephone service for residents. With the passage of the Telecommunications Act, "universal service" might be expanded to mean affordable telecommunications services for everyone, including every classroom, library, and health care facility.[16] This would broaden traditional entitlements beyond basic telephone service to include, for example, Internet access. It would also extend the scope of entitlement beyond residential customers to public facilities and, perhaps, nonprofit entities, such as schools and hospitals. While this may be a laudable goal and would undoubtedly benefit cities, it would definitely increase the cost of subsidies that would have to be borne by telecommunications providers and, ultimately, their customers. The task of determining the scope and entitlements of universal service has been delegated to a joint Federal-State Board.[17] Cities are not represented on the board and are, therefore, limited in their ability to influence these issues.

The universal service pool will require subsidies of approximately $12 billion.[18] The largest piece will be for residential rate assistance. One proposal has suggested that the pool should be funded by providers and resellers using a nondiscriminatory compensation structure, which would include various forms, including cash or in-kind services, such as network capacity, service offerings, and cooperative local infrastructure development.[19]

Another option for cities is to give providers access to public rights-of-way in exchange for universal service. Sunnyvale, for example, advocates that providers be required to maintain open networks as part of their existing common carrier obligations.[20] The city wants to lower encroachment fees as a bargaining tool, allowing private investors access to public rights-of-way at no or low cost.[21] By leveraging municipal resources and facilities, cities may be able to ensure that residents receive affordable telecommunications services, such as Internet access.

City Regulation of RTNs

Cities may regulate RTNs through their control over access to public rights-of-way and in exercise of their franchise authority. The major issue for cities as regulators is the extent to which they may impose annual fees or other charges on telecommunications providers, pursuant to their franchise authority. A franchise is "created when a governmental agency authorizes private companies to set up their infrastructures on public property in order to provide public utilities."[22] Electric, cable, telephone companies, and other public utilities are all subject to city franchise obligations, unless the state has preempted city authority, as is the case in California. Public utilities may also be subject to special taxes, such as utility user taxes. The issue for cities is whether the Act construes recurring franchise fees and taxes as entry barriers to competition and, therefore, unlawful or as reasonable compensation to cities for use of public rights-of-way, which is permissible.

Franchise Fee Obligations on Video Providers

Cities traditionally exercise local franchise authority over cable companies and other video providers by granting franchises. These franchises are adopted by city ordinance through a negotiated franchise agreement. The grant of a franchise neither precludes cities from building their own video delivery systems nor prevents cities from granting other franchises. The economics of the market, however, may make it infeasible to do so. Under cable franchise agreements, providers are generally required to pay annual franchise fees tied to a percentage of their gross revenues. In addition, cities may negotiate other concessions, such as public access channels.[23] For many cities, the revenue generated from franchise fees is a critical source of revenue for public services.

Sunnyvale, California, offers an example of the manner in which cities implement these franchise obligations. The city currently has franchise agreements for wireless communications with Metrocom and for cable TV services with TCI. Under these agreements, the franchisee pays the city five percent of gross revenues, which is deposited in the city's general fund.[24] The general fund is unrestricted and can be used by the city for any public purpose, including public improvements or other public projects.

The Telecommunications Act restricts a city's ability to extract compensation through franchise or other fees from cable companies seeking to diversify into new telecommunication services.[25] Cities, therefore, may neither leverage their franchise authority to force cable companies to provide additional capacity on their systems for city telecommunication services nor force a cable company to provide such services as a condition of granting or renewing their franchise. The only exception may be the sale of a franchise by a cable company, in which case it may be possible for a city to negotiate favorable concessions from the new cable company. For example, following the sale of a cable franchise by Viacom to TCI, Seattle began negotiating with TCI for favorable residential high-speed Internet access. As the city must approve any sales and may inquire into the public service to be provided by the new owner, it was able to leverage its authority to achieve additional concessions.

Just Compensation for Use of Rights-of-Way

The Telecommunications Act authorizes cities and the state PUCs to receive "just and reasonable" compensation for the use of their rights-of-way as well as for roof rights for wireless service providers.[26] These rights may not be unnecessarily withheld. Cities are permitted to establish such fees by negotiating contracts on a nondiscriminatory, competitively neutral basis. Once the fees have been established, they must be filed with the state PUC. The FCC and state PUCs have jurisdiction to review such fees, following a complaint that they are unreasonable.

The legislative history of Section 253 suggests that Congress intended cities to regulate the time or location of excavations to preserve traffic flow, prevent hazardous road conditions, and minimize noise impacts; to require that facilities be installed underground; and to enforce zoning regulations.[27] Moreover, any fees imposed would pertain to recovering street repair and paving costs and indemnity costs from personal injury claims arising from a company's excavation.

It seems clear that any fees imposed must be tied to actual or incremental costs or some related cost formula, rather than a revenue-based formula. Moreover, while there is no specific language stating that fees may be charged on an ongoing basis, the pole attachment provisions suggest that cities may be able to charge annual fees if they own and operate RTNs or own conduits or poles. The problem confronting many cities, including San Diego, is that they do not own existing utilities or facilities. While it is unclear exactly which actions by cities may be construed as entry barriers, the FCC has received petitions complaining that state and local taxes on utilities act as barriers.[28]

Franchise Fee Obligations on Public Utilities

Franchise requirements are generally imposed on any public utility, that is, entities that supply the inhabitants with light, water, power, heat, transportation, and telephone or other communications services. Telephone companies in some states, however, including California, have a statewide franchise that limits a city's ability to collect annual fees. This statewide franchise applies to all telephone companies operating within the state, even those that provide video and data services. This restriction does not apply to other public utilities, such as electric companies, nor does it preclude cities from imposing utility user taxes. For the purpose of telecommunications services, this disparity in imposing fees will likely be normalized, pursuant to the Telecommunications Act's prohibition against discriminatory treatment of telecommunications providers, by exempting all providers from paying annual fees tied to gross income.

Sunnyvale, California, proposes to create an advanced digital, broadband, telecommunications infrastructure.[29] Pacific Bell and the CAPs are exempt from local franchising requirements within California, including fees, but they must obtain encroachment permits for underground construction. The city, therefore, receives no franchise revenue from Pacific Bell or the CAPs. By contrast, the city also has an indefinite franchise agreement with Pacific Gas & Electric (PG&E) for gas and electric service, under which PG&E pays a franchise fee of one percent of gross revenues.[30] PG&E has unrestricted access to rights-of-way, although it must also obtain an encroachment permit, but it is not subject to the customer service standards imposed on TCI, the city's cable provider. In order to maximize a city's interest, it would need to be able to impose similar franchise requirements across all utility industries. The Telecommunications Act is likely to be interpreted to treat gas and electric companies providing telecommunications services more like cable and telephone companies, thereby exempting them from additional fees.

While some state PUCs, including the California Public Utilities Commission, preclude cities from collecting franchise fees from telephone companies, PUCs do allow telephone companies and other public utilities to assess annual, recurring fees[31] from entities that use their rights-of-way. This represents a disparity in rights to collect compensation for the use of the public versus private rights-of-way. In essence, these cities cannot collect annual franchise fees from telephone companies for the use of public streets, even though these same companies may charge others for access to their privately owned conduits. This raises the possibility that some cities will not receive franchise fees from resellers of LEC telecommunications services or others who interconnect with LECs.

Alternatives for Cities That Do Not Own Their Own Utilities

Cities have relied upon taxation and fees from telecommunications providers for revenue. Under the Telecommunications Act, these revenue sources are likely to be eliminated or restricted. As a result, cities must look for alternative sources to offset these losses. There are two alternative sources of revenue that may be available to cities that do not own municipal utility facilities, such as poles or conduits, or that are subject to statewide franchise restrictions. The first possibility is to build municipally owned conduits for public and private access. The second option is to impose utility user taxes on telecommunications providers.

Under the first option, cities would continue to process the permit applications of current carriers for access to existing private conduits or poles, until they reach capacity. Cities might then require that all new installation of lines or networks be through conduits that the city would install, maintain, or both. Such action would be based on a telecommunications policy that recognized the city's role as a facilitator or regulator to coordinate access and use of public rights-of-way. This strategy might be subject to legal challenge as a market entry barrier, if it precluded a carrier from engineering its network in the most technically and economically efficient manner.

Cities would be ill advised to restrict access to existing conduits. This restriction would likely constitute a "taking," requiring compensation by the government. A phased-in approach, however, would allow existing facilities to continue to operate, while cities address the likely proliferation of new telecommunications carriers and, therefore, the need to build new infrastructure conduits.

This approach might be justified on four grounds. First, cities have the authority, pursuant to their police powers, to coordinate access providers and to establish a process by which they may gain access to city rights-of-way. If all new cables or lines were passed through city-owned conduits, it would minimize the likely disruption to streets, which causes congestion and is a potential public hazard. Cities would be leasing space in their conduits, which is consistent with their rights as municipal utilities or telecommunications carriers.

Secondly, the Telecommunications Act clearly contemplated that interconnection for telecommunications services be implemented through a coordinated planning process.[32] The establishment of a process through city ordinance would minimize redundancy, maximize planning and coordination, and facilitate interconnectivity.

Third, as long as the rates were competitively neutral, nondiscriminatory, reasonable, and did not prohibit any telecommunications carrier from entering the market, there likely would be no basis for state or federal preemption. Finally, the LECs and cable companies would still be able to utilize their existing conduits for internal expansion or to lease space on their poles and conduits to third parties, until they reach capacity. As providers would still have a choice of whether to lease capacity in conduits from the city or from the LECs and cable companies, competition would not be restricted. These arguments would respond to likely challenges by LECs and cable companies that imposing requirements to use city-owned conduits would constitute a taking by the city, be discriminatory, or otherwise create an entry barrier.

Cities might also consider imposing taxes on use of utility services, which include public utilities, cable and telephone companies, and, arguably, telecommunications carriers. Sunnyvale imposes a utility user tax of 2 percent on all utilities, including PG&E and Pacific Bell.[33] In many instances, utilities collect the tax from users to give to the state, which then distributes the tax to cities on a proportional basis. Such taxes are authorized generally by Section 4223 of the Internal Revenue Code, but must also be specifically authorized in each state's constitution and under the city charter or authority. Utility user taxes are not specifically addressed by the Telecommunications Act of 1996.

While such taxes may not be viewed as market barriers, taxes generally are perceived by industry as disincentives to economic development. San Diego, for example, advertises the fact that it does not impose use taxes in order to attract businesses to the area. Consequently, imposing a utility user tax is recommended as a last alternative and only where there are other incentives to offset any adverse perception.

Conclusion

There is no question that regional telecommunications networks will develop and that cities will play critical roles in the process. The exact nature of the role will depend upon a variety of factors, including a city's resources, whether it owns its own utility, the amount of risk it is willing to assume, and the level of interest among existing and new providers in forming strategic partnerships. Cities should focus on developing strategic partnerships with each other and with other institutional users as leverage in negotiating favorable terms from providers.

For many cities, the uncertainty associated with technology may necessitate that cities use a combination of technologies to ensure that their networks may be interconnected and transparent. In addition, cities should concentrate on increasing the regional public services that may be offered on-line. This has the advantage of providing revenue for cities and enhancing their leverage as users in seeking partners to build their own regional networks. Moreover, since cities must still upgrade their existing private infrastructures, opportunities will be created to develop strategic partnerships with private industry. It may well be that it is too late for cities that do not already own a municipal utility to compete in the market to provide access to the public. It should not, however, deter cities from developing a telecommunications policy and actively exploring ways to benefit from their common use of the infrastructure to impact social and policy issues in the growth of regional telecommunications networks.

Notes

1. Virtual private networks service a city's internal or regional needs for governmental operations and administration. Examples include communication and data networks for libraries, schools, fire departments, police, and public works. Municipal Utilities are municipally owned public utilities that provide residents with telephone or other communications services and other public works, such as electric, gas, water, sewer, and/or other utility services.

2. RTN is a general term used to refer to municipal telecommunications networks that may cover one or more regions or cities within a state or between states and are interconnected at various points to enable the participating governments to

access and exchange information impacting the region or their common interests. An RTN may also provide public services in competition with private service providers.

3. "Telecommunications service" is defined as the "offering of telecommunications for a fee directly to the public, or to such classes of users as to be effectively available to the public, regardless of the facilities used." A "telecommunications carrier" includes any provider of information services on a common carrier basis, for a fee directly or indirectly to the public, without regard to the facilities used. Public Law 104, 153 (51).

4. Public Law 104, 251.

5. Public Law 104, 253.

6. City of Anaheim, "Anaheim City Council Approves Memorandum of Understanding with Spectranet to Build Fiber Optic Universal Telecommunications Systems," August 20, 1996, <http://www.anaheim.net/utility/telecom5.html>.

7. News Report No. DC 96-75, Action in CC Docket 96-98, August 1, 1996, <http://www.fcc.gov>.

8. Municipal utilities are exempt from regulation under the Pole Attachment Act. *Pole Attachment Act, U.S. Code,* Vol. 47, Sec. 224 (1984), California Public Utilities Code, Sec. 767.5 (a)(1).

9. *Ravettino v. San Diego,* 160 P. 2d 52, 56 (California Court of Appeals, 1945).

10. See the chapter in this volume by Lon Berquist and August E. Grant.

11. For example, the City of Austin, Texas, which operates a municipal utility, looked for a strategic partner to build an advanced telecommunications network. After two years and 34 respondents, Austin selected Central & South West Communications to build a hybrid fiber/coax network to interconnect all homes, businesses, and institutions. Ibid.

12. Ibid.

13. "Telecommunications Policy for the City of Sunnyvale, California", p. 20 (adopted February 1996), <http://reality.sgi.com/csp/sunnyvale/telecom.policy.html>.

14. San Diego Data Processing Corporation Request for Proposals to Provide Telecommunications Infrastructure (1995), p. 1.

15. Postalized rates are flat rate charges that are not based on distance. These rates are generally divided into interLata and intraLata rates, but are not based upon a per mile distance. Inter and intra-Lata are geographical boundaries used to identify the service markets for local exchange carriers. In some instances, these rates may also include flat rates not tied to the per minute or per usage units typically found in switched lines. Interview with Fredric Goldberg, Senior Network Architect, NASA Lewis Research Center (December 27, 1996).

16. Public Law 104, 254.

17. Public Law 104, 254 (b).

18. "Statement of Reed E. Hundt, Chairman, Federal Communications Commission, on Implementation of the Telecommunications Act of 1996 before the Subcommittee on Telecommunications and Finance Committee on Commerce, U.S. House of Representatives," July 18, 1996, p. 7, <http://www.fcc.gov/Reports/reh71896.html>.

19. Brenda J. Trainor, Manager, Regional Telecommunications, Clark County, Nevada, "The Local Government Perspective: Can the Harmonica Play in the Symphony?" Presented December 6, 1995, at New York Law School's Conference, "Universal Service in Context: A Multidisciplinary Perspective," p. 4, <http://cdinet.com/Benton/Retrieve/Univ-service1.txt>.

20. "Telecommunications Policy for the City of Sunnyvale, California," November 6, 1995, p. 20.

21. Encroachment fees are fees imposed by cities for the privilege of digging up city streets and rights-of-way.

22. *Saathoff v. City of San Diego*, 35 Cal. App. 4th 697, 703, 41 Cal. Rptr. 2d 352, 356 (1995).

23. *Cable Act of 1984, U.S. Code*, Vol. 47, Sec. 543 (1988).

24. "Telecommunications Policy for the City of Sunnyvale," pp. 12–13.

25. Public Law 104, 303.

26. Public Law 104, 253.

27. "In the Matter of Classical Telephone," 11 FCCR 13082, 1996 FCC Lexis 5414, 5446 (October 1, 1996).

28. Remarks of Blair Levin, Chief of Staff, Federal Communication Commission, at 61st Annual Conference of the International Municipal Lawyers Association, Little Rock, Arkansas, October 7, 1996.

29. "Telecommunications Policy for the City of Sunnyvale," p. 6.

30. Ibid.

31. In California, for example, the annual fee for pole attachment is $2.50 in the first year. Thereafter, the annual fee is $2.50 or 7.4 percent of the public utility's annual cost of ownership for the pole and supporting anchor.

32. Public Law 104, 256.

33. "Telecommunications Policy for the City of Sunnyvale," p. 12.

Power on Both Sides Now: The Critical Role of Electric Utilities in Internet Development

Steven R. Rivkin

Users of the Internet are not able to benefit from its full bounty of information because markets and public policy have not yet found ways to deliver more than a trickle of the potential that state-of-the-art telecommunications can provide. How may activated citizens, on their own and with allies, break through the barriers to freer flows of information? The task of this chapter is to sketch the electric utilities' critical piece in this puzzle.

Given the size and pervasiveness of the venerable electric power industry and its own increasing dependence on real-time information, the industry and the dynamic young Internet are doubtless heading, to borrow from Franklin Roosevelt, for a "rendezvous with destiny."[1] In the process, both are sure to benefit from a mutuality that builds upon size as well as logic. The statistics underline the preeminence of electric utilities. Their revenues exceeded $173 billion in 1994 (more than the communications industries), and they serve 97 percent of American homes (a percentage point more than telephone companies and more than 30 points greater than cable television).[2]

In essence, the presence of electric service in virtually every home matches precisely the potential universal penetration of the Internet. Moreover, the $821 average annual residential power bill[3] posts a handsome reward for saving electricity and money through information. Reducing costs of this magnitude creates a focused challenge, with a handy reward for innovation.

For this challenge, the Internet's functional importance is its ability to enlist on-line participants in informed and rational behavior, limited only by the scale of actual penetration and available bandwidth. In theory, at least, there are huge affinities between the electric utility and the Internet.

But, in practice, the first 100 feet is still a huge gap that utilities and consumers must conquer before they may grasp those affinities. Many utilities are preoccupied with wrenching transformations of their own, posed by industry restructuring and competition. But, before long, information strategies will help many utilities to survive and some to prosper. Utilities will be able to build on the power of their incumbency, although some incumbents will also be menaced by their new competitors' own information reach. As the electric industry moves from monopolies to more competition, the ability to utilize information in dealings with customers may well become the margin of competitive success. Eventually, the electric industry as a whole may embrace information-based strategies so vigorously that it will take the lead in breaking the barriers to widely available broadband telecommunications.

This chapter outlines a scenario in which utilities might now take that lead by creating "common infrastructure"—telecommunications facilities to be built and leased by utilities to other service providers, saving bandwidth for the utilities' own communications with power customers. The chapter first discusses changes in the electric industry that are driving utilities to rely on broadband telecommunications. Next, the utilities' "negative incentive," if they fail to do so, is considered—the possibility that customers using Internet access of their own to interact with competitive rivals might break free from the local utility's grasp. Finally, the essentials of "common infrastructure" are explored, along with its timely significance for the nation as a whole, not just for the power companies.

From Indifference to Enthusiasm

Until very recently, most utilities cared surprisingly little about opportunities in telecommunications. They had invested billions of dollars in communications networks to control their own operations, which became especially critical after a regionwide blackout crippled the eastern United States in the mid-1960s. Eventually, the magnitude of investment that utilities made in telecommunications placed them second only to the telephone industry in the value of telecommunications plant investment.

Historically, relationships between telecommunications and electricity providers were virtually nonexistent, despite their physical proximity. The linkages that existed were never more than casual. For example, it is only in the last few years that utilities have seen value in disposing of surplus "dark fiber" in their electric transmission facilities via leases to long-distance telephone companies.[4] Meanwhile, "local-loop" telephone companies hewed to a tradition of strict self-reliance—relying on their own batteries to store up electricity in their telephone exchanges to power copper telephone networks and drive signaling devices, contending that commercial electric service was too erratic.

Notably, Thomas Edison made fundamental discoveries that launched both the electric and telecommunications industries. Such facilities as poles and conduits were often shared and the base of ultimate customers was identical, yet services developed in complete separation, probably because electromagnetic radiation menaces electronic telecommunications.[5] More recently, all physical justification for this separation disappeared with the advent of fiber optics for telecommunications. Now, both messages and electricity can even be carried on a single medium, a "composite cable" on which messages pass optically right through an electric field.

Utilities, for their part, have long known that the standard watt-hour meter measuring electricity consumption at the residence imposes enormous economic burdens of low "load factors." Generating and transmission capacity is often idled to accommodate fluctuating demands. Such meters, installed in virtually every residence in North America and completely amortized long ago, measure energy in constant units, regardless of when consumption occurs. Unlike other facilities-scarce industries, which drive demand toward supply by varying prices, electric utilities were not able to use rates to induce consumers to consume more efficiently. Although frequent remote readings via telecommunications might enable prices to be set dynamically, utilities have chosen to avoid this dependence on telecommunications, even though it might reduce the enormous financial and, incidentally, environmental burdens of overcapacity in power supply and transmission.

The indifference of utilities extended to one instance in which a utility, faced with the need to claim an electricity-related purpose to gain permission from the U.S. Securities & Exchange Commission to acquire a lucrative cable television franchise, deliberately refused to "play the efficiency card."[6] The utility believed that a claim that it might need two-way telecommunications to meter and price electricity would ultimately shatter its historically comfortable regulatory isolation.

All that has changed now, with the imminent disaggregation of the vertically integrated electric utility, driving every power company in the United States to reevaluate its specific liabilities and future market prospects. Key regulatory milestones have been the advent of mandatory open access for competitive wholesale generation, which the Federal Energy Regulatory Commission ordered in 1996;[7] comparable initiatives to accomplish "retail wheeling" (open access to competing sellers, ultimately reaching the individual residence), which are pending in almost every state; and the filing in Congress of several bills to federalize and preempt the process of retail wheeling to make it uniform nationwide.

While there is no certainty as to the pace, timing, and scope of restructuring, there is a huge and economically significant ferment in Washington and state capitals about it. Although it is mostly conceded that the traditional vertically integrated electric monopoly will eventually end, the nature of the resulting markets remains unclear.

Many informed observers expect that power generation will be competitive, with some individual residences even becoming both suppliers and consumers of energy (via new microsources of "distributed" energy, such as turbines, fuel cells, and solar collectors, which will need to be linked electronically). Transmission may become more oligopolistic, neither wholly competitive nor wholly monopolistic, and local distribution will probably remain a monopoly. Since patterns will vary across the country and various well-financed interests will fight furiously for advantage, even this forecast is uncertain.

The significance for Internet and broadband development of these developments in the electric industry is indirect, but nevertheless real and substantial. In the first place, many investor-owned electric utilities, traditionally combining generation, transmission, and distribution in one contiguous territory, face huge losses from electricity competition. They will need to write off an estimated $135 billion[8] in obsolete plants, whose electric output may easily be underpriced by competition.

Suppliers of cheaper electricity are itching to take customers away from unfortunately situated high-cost producers. The latter, for their part, are entreating legislators and regulators to delay competition or otherwise to mandate that ratepayers pay off incumbents' "stranded costs" before the utilities get knocked to bits by competition.

This struggle has several telecommunications and information ramifications. First, low-cost producers and power marketers will have to communicate with the ultimate customer in order to market their cheaper energy. In 1996, the Federal Energy Regulatory Commission ordered that such contacts be conducted in accordance with the open protocols of the Internet,[9] thereby laying a logical foundation for future retail markets to operate over the Internet as well.

Secondly, distribution entities, the parts of power companies likely to remain local monopolies when vertical disaggregation is complete, will try to communicate defensively and creatively with local customers, counting on historical loyalties to enable them to maximize their share of the customer's total energy bill. Otherwise, competing suppliers of "energy services" will try to capture value and marginalize the functional significance and value of the services of the local distributor.

These two points are complementary. Some utilities will want to use telecommunications and information to capture customers, while others will use the same tools to retain their customers. One study indicated that as much as $35 billion a year in potential cost reductions to the consumer, savings available for infrastructure investments, or some combination of the two, will be at stake in this information-based struggle.[10]

Finally, to the extent that politicians slow down utility disaggregation to permit the partial or full recovery of "stranded costs," many utilities will be awash in cash. Until such deals are securely done, though, the utilities seeking political relief will not risk untimely embarrassment by making flashy new investments in telecommunications. Nevertheless, assurance of future recoveries will facilitate their later investments in capital-consuming telecommunications plant. Already, many utilities are readying themselves for such major redeployments.[11]

The situation is changing now, from genuine indifference to guarded enthusiasm and more, with regard to telecommunications' future role in utilities and the utilities' provision of telecommunications services. For reasons rooted in their own structural imperatives, electric utilities are becoming formidable, indeed indispensable, participants in future infrastructure development and the delivery of information services.

Paths to the Meter

The central concern for the utility is the residential electric meter, which cannot measure time-of-use until it is supplemented with a telecommunications linkup and home information storage, processing, and manipulation. Adding these enhancements is tantamount to building the infrastructure needed for the Internet, both local area networks (LANs) within the house and wide-area networks (WANs) to central computers, with implications extending far beyond utility applications.

Achieving this so-called customer interface requires transformations of both technology and marketing methods, in order to motivate more efficient and conserving customer behavior. Once the utility attains the ability to set prices that fluctuate according to time of use, those prices may be varied in shorter and shorter intervals, until eventually real-time pricing is achieved. The more sophisticated the pricing, the more extensive the telecommunications and computing capacity deployed by the utility in the residence.

There are two main scenarios by which these transformations may occur. One might be called a "trickle-up" scenario, meaning the gradual enhancement by residential consumers, on their own or working with a power provider, to open up narrowband information linkages between the consumer and the power provider. A competing approach might be called the "cascade-down" scenario, with the deliberate expansion by the local utility of its distribution lines of business to include broadband infrastructure.

The first scenario—consumer empowerment—is typified by two demonstration projects recently initiated with financial support from the U.S. Department of Energy's Office of Energy Research and technical support from Los Alamos National Laboratory.

In San Diego, a group of 50 homes were slated to receive high-speed Internet service, coupled with interactive access to the website of San Diego Gas and Electric, via Pacific Bell's existing 750 megahertz hybrid fiber-coax system. This project aimed to make the power company's Internet site its primary vehicle for demand-side management, regardless of the bandwidth available.

A second demonstration project in Laredo, Texas, also sponsored by the Department of Energy with CSW Communications (a subsidiary of Central & South West Corporation, a utility holding company) planned to connect 50 to 100 broadband customers to an operating, utility-owned, hybrid fiber-coax plant, also providing up to 100 other customers with dial-in access. Several schools and institutions would also have been connected. All these customers were to be linked to CSW's existing energy management services and to the Internet. The project sought to demonstrate the feasibility of electric utilities becoming Internet and energy service providers.

In both projects, access would have been achieved over available broadband facilities (in San Diego provided by the phone company, and in Laredo by the utility itself), but the broadband capabilities were not critical in the test phase. Both projects, however, have unfortunately been abandoned without demonstrable results, in large part due to shifts in priorities by the companies involved.[12] Both projects would have enhanced the utility's ability to interact with its own consumers and also to reach out to consumers in adjacent utility territories, or anywhere, to market energy directly to them.

It will be a two-way street, as far as power companies and the Internet are concerned. Customers with a personal computer and a modem will be able to reach out and buy power at the cheapest price from any source, anywhere in the United States, and maybe Canada and Mexico eventually, and compel the local utility to deliver electricity or gas for nothing more than freight charges. By virtue of the Internet, the customer will no longer be tied to the local power company.

The full threat to utilities is reflected in a June 1996 item in the *New York Times*, announcing a patent granted for a box that fits on a residential telephone and, before long-distance dialing is completed, automatically inventories as many as 867 carriers' rate plans to choose the cheapest path.[13] The same could happen for electricity purchases.

Reinventing the Electric Utility

In the second scenario, the local utilities will build the broadband infrastructure themselves. The utility may reinvent itself by expanding horizontally, just when broken up vertically, thereby responding adroitly to new competitive pressures and technological opportunities. Electric utilities can now build the networks needed, run them on a natural monopoly basis, contrary to popular opinion,[14] and make truly robust competition possible in telecommunications services. Indeed, it may be that the "natural monopoly" nature of local broadband fiber networks is the real reason that they have not yet been widely deployed. Utilities may thereby build platforms from which cable companies, telephone companies, and others may offer advanced services far faster and with less risk than they might on a competitive basis.

As competition in electricity supply drives local utilities to defend their foremost assets, their customer bases, a critical advantage will be the ability to reach all customers through a broadband system, in "real time," with state-of-the-art energy management. The challenge, therefore, that may transform and save today's electric utilities will be to bring about that broadband capability, assure themselves priority in its use, and exploit it aggressively to defend their core business. While media other than broadband may be useful and cost-efficient, it is presently the case that power marketers that use broadband as it becomes available will have an advantage over rivals that do not.

In developing a broadband communications infrastructure, utilities would do best to follow a collaborative strategy, which may permit them to do very well indeed. In order to enlist information and telecommunications providers as partners, rather than rivals, utilities should first give up the prospect of attempting to compete with them in retail services. Then, by building the enabling infrastructure, the local utility will be shrewdly positioned to stake its own claim to be the preferred provider of information-based energy services for its own residential customers.

Passing up the rumored pot of gold in competitive telecommunications challenges conventional wisdom. Nevertheless, there is a far greater virtue to be made of the necessity for the utility to lead incumbent cable and telephone companies and other information providers into a joint endeavor, which would also make the utility more secure in its core business of providing electricity.

The utility, therefore, would position itself in telecommunications as an independent entity not in competition with information service providers. It would support service providers' needs to get community-wide facilities up and running faster than they could themselves, largely because they are presently poised only to struggle against each other. The choice for incumbents should be logical and beyond much hesitation: the assurance of a comfortable niche from which to start selling tomorrow's high-value services—right now—and the rejection of the endless struggle that would necessitate building facilities first, at huge costs, before earning a dime of revenue.

In fact, incumbents in telecommunications have historically preferred to accommodate potential rivals rather than to pursue ruinous, facilities-based competition. At least four times since the Civil War, new infrastructure has come into being in the United States through accommodation—potential competitors found ways to differentiate services and allocate markets.[15]

By passing up unrealistic hopes to become retail players, alert utilities stand to gain a vitally important and vastly more secure role in telecommunications, building and managing a natural monopoly in local transport according to a model called "common infrastructure."

The place to start should be promoting local consensus among incumbents and regulators about the utility's future supporting role. In dedicating itself to both enabling equal access and providing universal service in telecommunications, familiar requisites of electric service, the utility would address critical, unsolved flaws in public policy, to its immense political credit. But with or without consensus, the utility would likely set off a chain reaction that would realign roles and hasten decisions by erstwhile competitors, simply by declaring its intentions to "thicken" its energy transmission and distribution functions to include telecommunications transport.

A metaphor from commercial real estate is helpful. Similarly to the developer of a shopping mall, the utility would build a common facility, which its tenants would customize by installing their own switches and residential gateways to serve ultimate customers. Major strategic partners, specifically including local cable and telephone companies, would become "anchor tenants" under long-term priority leases, reflecting their places in today's markets, their capital investments in older networks, and their franchised service obligations. So as to abide by the antitrust laws, other specialty tenants would have rights to lease slots on common infrastructure, up to the limit of the fiber-optic facility's expandable capacity.

There are instructive precedents for deciding the rents. Initial tenants generally are well rewarded for taking on greater risks. Rents sometimes fall as occupancy, that is, competition, builds up. Landlords usually share in gross receipts. The shopping center model suggests that, led by a developer's initiative, competitors may all thrive in each other's presence by gaining swift and sure access to the maximum possible number of customers.

Other analogies are encouraging. Economists write about the "network externalities" of a telephone system, meaning that the system becomes more valuable as its subscribers proliferate. Thus, deliberately building up both competitors and customers makes for great business. Such dynamism contrasts sharply with the inherent poverty of the present strict-competition model, by which essential facilities have yet to be built.

In becoming the hinge on which a grand realignment in local telecommunications would turn, the utility would reap obvious economic and political rewards. But it would also be well situated to claim for itself, or an affiliate, the anchor tenancy in its own special sector of energy management, thereby building a preemptive edge against competitors that threaten its customer base.

All the present "incumbents," telephone, cable, and utility companies, might try to get a head start against competition by jointly maximizing the near-term value of their "brand" reputations and ongoing relationships with customers. But, new competitors would also share functionally equal chances under the antitrust laws to make their own ingenious assaults on universal markets that the electric utility's initiative would open up to all competitors.

Partners Together

The electric utility is the incumbent best positioned to round up anchor tenants and to develop common infrastructure as a private, commercial initiative. There is a compelling logic to this path. Once tenants sign letters of intent to lease facilities, the developer may secure project financing privately, using the lease contracts as collateral rather than the future bills of captive rate-payers or the credit of any municipality. Traditional government regulation and financing, therefore, would not be needed or appropriate.

Two linked, competitive reasons should now drive all incumbents—electric, telephone, and cable providers—to recognize that they had best work together to develop telecommunications. First, the longer incumbents anguish over how to redefine themselves in the face of oncoming competition, the greater the likelihood that their "brand" identifications will erode and their customers will go elsewhere. Getting a universal broadband system up and running will allow incumbents some lead-time to reorganize and retain their customers.

Secondly, the incredible potency of the Internet suggests that consumers armed with personal computers and modems may soon snatch away the lion's share of the value of any product or service that they consume at home. This potential for consumer autonomy via the Internet will enable information technology to crush local utilities and telecommunications firms alike, unless they decide to work together, led by the fortuitously well-placed electric utility, to deploy common infrastructure now.

Notes

1. Franklin D. Roosevelt, speech accepting renomination as president of the United States, June 27, 1936.

2. U.S. Department of Commerce, *Statistical Abstract of the United States—1995: The National Data Book* (Washington, DC: U.S. Department of Commerce, Bureau of the Census, 1995), Table 700, p. 452; Table 897, p. 571; Table 980, p. 605; and Table 904, p. 574.

3. Ibid., Table 970, p. 605.

4. According to a 1993 estimate prepared by the Industry Analysis Division of the Federal Communications Commission (FCC), interexchange carriers had installed "over 100,000 fiber miles (4,700 miles of cable) within electric utility rights-of-way (e.g., buried next to transmission towers) throughout the country." Testimony of Michael Katz, FCC Chief Economist, before Subcommittees on Telecommunications and Finance and Energy and Power, House Committee on Energy and Commerce, July 29, 1994, p. 4.

5. The technological, economic, and legal history of this separation of facilities and services a century ago merits exploration by a competent historian of science.

6. *Mississippi Power & Light Company*, 1982, Fed. Sec. Rep. (CCH), Sec. 77, 241.

7. U.S. Federal Energy Regulatory Commission Order 888, "Open Access Non-Discriminatory Transmission Services," *Federal Register* 61 (May 10, 1996): 21540.

8. Estimate of Moody's Investors Service, quoted in Benjamin A. Holden, "Shift to Deregulation May Cost Electricity Industry $135 Billion," *Wall Street Journal*, August 7, 1995, p. B4.

9. U.S. Federal Energy Regulatory Commission Order 889. "Open Access Same-Time Information System," *Federal Register* 61 (May 10, 1996): 21737.

10. Anderson Consulting LLP, "The Role of Broadband Communications in the Utility of the Future" (1995), p. 22.

11. "Electrical Utilities Telecom Ventures—Partial List," *New Technology Week*, September 2, 1997, p. 8.

12. The cancellation of the San Diego and Laredo projects is greatly overshadowed by the more recent and successful launch in Tacoma, Washington, of a $100 million broadband network project by Tacoma City Light, the municipal utility. City Light broke ground in early 1998, over the objections of the incumbent cable operator, in a daring network-building initiative primarily justified by its value as a medium for energy management and marketing. See John Healey, "The People's Wires," *Governing*, August 1997, and "Some Local Cheers for Creeping Socialism," *New York Times*, October 4, 1997, p. B1.

13. "A Little Box Holds Out the Enticing Promise of the Lowest Long-Distance Rate Every Time You Call," *New York Times*, July 17, 1997, p. C6.

14. The mainstream definition of "natural monopoly" fits local broadband networks, where the incumbent can serve an additional customer through an

existing facility more cheaply than a rival can build a competing facility. This assumes that wireless is not a substitute for broadband fiber, except in limited circumstances. Also, the potential of utilities' existing distribution lines to carry in excess of one megabit per second, recently demonstrated in England (see *Wall Street Journal*, October 9, 1997, p. B21, and *Wall Street Journal*, March 25, 1998, p. A10), would defeat this conclusion, if proven in contemplated field tests.

15. Such market-splitting decisions are substantiated historically by the following instances: Western Union and the Associated Press in 1867, Western Union and the Bell Company in 1879, and AT&T and RCA in 1926. Likewise, a generation ago, cable television emerged—its battles notwithstanding—in a nonthreatening niche between broadcasters and telephone companies. See R. Horowitz, *The Irony of Regulatory Reform: The Deregulation of American Telecommunications* (New York: Oxford University Press, 1989), p. 94, 97, and 116–117.

Utilities Unleashed: An Answer to Customers' Internet and Broadband Service Needs

Bernice K. McIntyre

Our global society demands that all individuals, regardless of their location or income, and every business, whatever its size, be connected to advanced communications networks in order to find employment opportunities, create markets for business products, and compete effectively. This requirement applies equally to agrarian areas, where the world commodity price of products must be known when the fields are being harvested, and to urban schools, which are preparing children to compete for jobs in a global market. While access to the necessary information may be provided by a combination of satellite-based products, wireless technologies, radio, video and wireline technologies, these networks and infrastructures must be connected and configured to give users transparent and effective access. These advanced communications services must also be affordably priced and ubiquitously available, in order to provide these benefits universally.

Utilities as Access and Communications Providers

Utilities are naturally suited to help realize the vision of ubiquitous, affordable, advanced communications infrastructure and services to the home for five reasons. First, utilities have the incentive to strengthen their contacts with their customers, a majority of which are residential customers. Secondly, utilities have the communications infrastructure to provide access to these services. Third, they can reach all customers, since they have traditionally had greater penetration rates than communications companies. Fourth, they have the technical capability and core competencies necessary to provide these services. Finally, the regulatory environment now permits them to provide the services. There are many examples among both publicly and privately owned utilities that demonstrate utilities' interest in pursuing new opportunities for providing advanced telecommunications services to their customers. We can only hope that regulators clear the path and enable utilities to explore fully the opportunities to meet their customers needs in these new markets.

Communications Infrastructure

Utilities already have extensive communications infrastructures. Use of these assets avoids the cost of building redundant, duplicative facilities, which keeps societal costs of the network lower than they might otherwise be. Utilities know how to operate sophisticated microwave, telephone, fiber-optic, two-way radio and/or computer circuits for internal purposes. They have the right to access roads and equipment on poles via rights-of-way. Local and state officials have granted these rights-of-way to utilities to enable them to operate their transmission and distribution networks. Utilities own a significant portion of the nation's fiber cable and microwave spectrum, which are two technological mediums for providing broadband services. Utilities already lease some of the fiber cable to communications service providers for this purpose.

As stated in a report prepared for UTC, an international trade association representing the telecommunications interests of organizations involved in the production, transportation or distribution of electric power, gas or water, "Utilities' core operations rely on extensive telecommunications technologies for reading meters, providing and obtaining customer information and feedback, identifying and solving problems, and billing."[1] These communications-dependent systems include remote appliance control, information feedback to utilize energy at off-peak hours, automatic meter reading, and transmission of price information to customers, such as real-time pricing, automatic billing, and electronic funds transfers. Utilities rely on communications-based technologies to control the operations of their transmission and distribution networks. One of these communications-dependent tools is the supervisory control data acquisition system (SCADA).

Utilities also use microwave systems for employee dispatch and other internal operational needs. Utilities have invested over $4.3 billion in private radios and $1.3 billion in point-to-point microwave stations.[2]

One example of this kind of interaction between utilities and communications is presented by Intelcom, one of the largest providers of competitive local telecommunications service in the United States, which forms partnerships with utility companies and leverages their communications assets to provide new services. Intelcom has a twenty-five-year contract with Southern California Edison to lease 1,200 miles of fiber and similar arrangements with the City Public Service of San Antonio, Texas. It leases twenty-two miles of fiber network from the Southern Company in Birmingham, Alabama.[3] Simply by building upon existing utility assets, Intelcom will have a larger fiber-optic network than MCI and many other competitive access providers (see Table 1).

Similarly, in 1994 AT&T had 41,664 route miles of fiber, of which 28,656 fiber miles were provided by electric utilities.[4] Since fiber mile is equal to the number of miles of each cable multiplied by the number of strands in the cable, it is not possible to determine the percentage of AT&T's fiber network that is provided by electric utilities. The Federal Communications Commission (FCC) is beginning to collect this information.

Penetration

As a result of their monopoly history, electric utilities and water utilities have nearly 100 percent penetration in their franchise areas. This high penetration rate is one of the fundamental reasons that long-distance telephone carriers, interested in providing local exchange and other services, seek partnerships with utilities. For example, RCN, a subsidiary of LDDS WorldCom, has a joint venture and partnership with Boston Edison, an electric utility providing service to metropolitan Boston, to provide Internet and other broadband services to the public. Potomac Electric and

Table 1   Route Miles at the End of 1995

Company	Route Miles
Teleport Communications Group, Inc. (TCG)	5,065
MFS Communications Company , Inc. (MFS)	2,903
MCI Metro	2,338
Intelcom	3,000

Source: Telecom Publishing Group, "Utilities on Telecom: A New Source of Power," Vol. 2, p. 30, 1996.

Power Company, an electric distribution company in the Washington, DC area, also has a similar arrangement with RCN. These utilities provide RCN with access to fiber miles and customers, allowing RCN to enter new markets rapidly.

Incentives for Utilities

Utilities have many incentives to provide new types of services to existing customers. The U.S. utility industry is facing competitive forces that require both gas and electric utilities to market their services to their customers in order to retain them. Over the past decade, the gas industry has been deregulated and is no longer vertically integrated. Gas production is separated from distribution and transmission. Pipeline companies no longer own gas wells or distribute gas to retail customers, and retail gas distribution companies may buy gas from any source and have it delivered through the pipeline transmission system. Gas has become a true commodity. Many believe that electricity is moving in the same direction.

The United States Congress is considering legislation that would restructure the electric industry. A bill first introduced in the 104th Congress by Congressman Dan Schaeffer would give "all American electricity consumers the right to choose among competitive providers of electricity in order to secure lower electricity rates, higher quality services, and a more robust United States economy."[5] The U.S. Department of Energy under former Secretary of Energy Federico Peña also considered the issue of customer choice and electric utility restructuring and introduced proposed legislation in 1998.[6] This movement toward more competitive utility markets is forcing utility executives to reassess their core business. Some utilities are choosing to divest themselves of all their generation assets as a first step in preparing for the restructured electric utility industry. As part of a settlement process in Massachusetts, New England Electric System divested itself of its generation assets in exchange for recovery of its sunk costs in the transition to a more competitive market.[7] As electric utilities become less involved in the generation market, and more dependent upon their wires as their priority service obligation and source of revenue, new uses of these wires will be contemplated. The provision of broadband services is one of many applications that are presently being considered and undertaken in the industry.

Customer service will be increasingly important in maintaining customer loyalty to utility companies as they face competition. Internet and other broadband services that rely upon utilities' infrastructure provide one way for utilities to enhance their services. In fact, publicly owned utilities are already providing such value-added services for their customers, as discussed below.

There are also profit incentives for utilities to enter these new markets. For example, the New England energy market is mature, growing at less than one-half of one percent each year.[8] Utility executives are searching for new markets that are related to their core capabilities and business and that offer potential high returns for their rate payers and shareholders. Internet service is a high-growth market.

Core Competencies

The attributes that businesses seek in an Internet provider correspond to the core competencies that most utilities have developed, are in the process of developing, or will be required to develop to survive in the restructured competitive markets (see Table 2).

The competitive gas market requires gas utilities to be highly accountable to their customers or risk losing them. For example, pipelines must offer choice to their retail customers in order to be effective gas traders. Enron, one of the largest integrated natural gas and electricity companies in the world,[9] provides communica-

Table 2   The Fit between Commercial Internet Users and Utilities

Commercial Internet Users' Needs*	Utility Companies' Core Competencies
Reliable service	Ubiquitous reliability is a core competency
Available service	Ubiquitous availability is a core competency
Accountability	A future core competency
Provider choice	A future core competency
Security/privacy	Network security is a core competency
Transparency	A future core competency
Value-added services	Energy efficiency is a value-added service

*Modified from Daniel Dern, "Meeting the Challenges of Business and End Users Communities on the Internet: What They Want, What They Need, What They're Doing," in Brian Kahin and James Keller, eds., *Public Access to the Internet* (Cambridge, MA: MIT Press, 1995), pp. 212–213.

tions services to its customers and has also entered the electricity commodity trading business.[10]

The electric industry is moving in the same direction. Already more than 110 investment dealers, utilities and energy traders have obtained licenses to market power from the Federal Energy Regulatory Commission (FERC).[11] By 2002, transparency of service will be among the core competencies of most electric utilities, so that they may provide transmission access for wholesale and, in many states, retail wheeling. (Wheeling is the transportation of power over a third-party transmission or distribution network to enable either wholesale or retail power sales and purchases.) Utilities will be using communications, telephony and data systems to serve a new commodity market in electrons. The transfer of electrons may or may not be on the Internet, but it will be on a private data network supported by a very sophisticated communications infrastructure.

If utilities will be using these sophisticated information services to buy and sell power, to wheel and to ensure reliability of electric power service, why not offer their distribution customers the same sophisticated packages of services?

The highly competitive, fast pace of the video, Internet and broadband service marketplaces would be challenging to a regulated industry accustomed to earning a return on assets as a matter of course. The electric industry, however, is encountering its own revolution and must adapt to the changes that restructuring will bring. The restructuring of the electric utility industry and the introduction of competition will force utilities to try to differentiate their services from their competitors to survive. Competitive forces will also drive utilities toward an ever greater sensitivity to customer service.

Demand side management (DSM) and efficiency programs that reduce the peak load and control the time of use of appliances have also helped utilities learn about the usage patterns of their customers. These programs were one of the first applications for communications technologies that connected directly with customers, particularly residential and small business customers. These services and others related to remote meter reading, billing and collection can use the Internet and broadband services as a vehicle for continued development of strong customer relations and provide enhanced mechanisms for customer contact.

Since utilities own communications facilities, including pole attachments, rights-of-way, dark fiber and spectrum, they may participate in the communications marketplace at a variety of levels and the societal cost of their entering the market may be lower than that of most other new entrants. They may act as access providers, by providing their rights-of-way or poles or by leasing their dark fiber to other carriers. They may serve as a back office, helping Internet service providers, telephony providers, and others with billing, collections, and other services. Through equity ownership in other companies or direct provision of services, they may actually provide the new broadband services. The role that utilities choose rests in part on the utilities' view of their core business and capabilities in the twenty-first century as well as the business risks involved in market entry. Part of the business risk is determined by public policy. Will state and federal regulators encourage utilities to participate fully in this new market or will they discourage utilities from doing so? The answer rests in part on whether public policy leaders regard full participation by utilities as a benefit to society or an overriding detriment to ratepayers.

The Regulatory Environment

Congress removed the barriers to entry to the communications market for utilities, on the one hand, by prohibiting any local or state government from creating barriers to entry to the market and, on the other hand, by allowing registered utility holding companies to participate in the market through the use of "exempt telecommunications companies."[12]

It has been stated elsewhere that "the 1996 Telecommunications Act should prevent any state or local government from prohibiting any entity from providing interstate or intrastate telecommunications services. This development represents an unfettered opportunity for local utility companies to enter the market."[13] But, it remains to be seen whether the 1996 Telecommunications Act (the Act) will actually provide this opportunity.

The Act specifically prohibits state and local government from blocking entry in the interstate or intrastate telecommunications services market.[14] The Act permits a specific class of utility companies, registered utility holding companies, to provide telecommunications services, information services, and other services and products, subject to FCC jurisdiction, without the cumbersome approval processes previously required by the Securities and Exchange Commission (SEC). This class of utilities may form "exempt telecommunications companies" (ETCs) to provide these services. The ETC assignation is inappropriate because the Act does not exempt these companies from all regulation. The companies are still rightfully subject to the jurisdiction of state commissions and the Federal Energy Regulatory Commission, but they are exempted from the approval processes of the SEC. Prior to the passage of the Act, any investment by a registered utility company in a nonutility business, including telecommunications, necessitated a specific finding by the SEC that the new business was functionally related to the traditional business and was consistent with the operation of an integrated public utility system.

Even prior to the passage of the Act, however, the SEC had approved several telecommunications subsidiaries and found them to have the required "functional relationship" to the utility business. The SEC approved:

• Southern Company's acquisition of ICS Integrated Systems, Inc., a computer software company for two-way communications over local telephone lines (1984);

• the American Electric Power (AEP) purchase of 15 percent of ICS (1987);

• AEP subsidiaries' lease of over half their fiber networks to nonassociated companies, with the revenue to be applied to the costs of the network (1988);

• the acquisition by Entergy of an interest in First Pacific Networks for a communications system with DSM applications (1991);

• the formation by Central and South West (CSW) of a nonutility subsidiary that would lease half of CSW's fiber network to nonassociated companies (1994);

• the leasing to nonaffiliated companies of some of GPU's retail subsidiaries' fiber networks constructed for internal purposes (1994); and

• the investment by Southern Company of over $179 million in Southern Communications to install and operate a communications system throughout Georgia, Alabama, northwestern Florida, and southeastern Mississippi (1995).[15]

These SEC approvals prior to the adoption of the Act are evidence that the link between utility services and communications may be not only consistent with the provision of utility services, but may also be a core function of providing these services. The Act clears the way for utilities to plumb this new market further.

Utilities' Activities Today to Meet Customer Needs

Both privately and publicly owned utilities have been exploring the use of their internal communications networks to enhance service to their customers.

Many investor-owned utilities are making investments in their communications infrastructures, partnering with other companies to provide communications services, leasing communications facilities, or expanding the use of their communications infrastructure to provide energy management or communications services.

Almost all these efforts involve some use of fiber optics or other broadband technologies. The number of utilities making investments in fiber optics is increasing, as companies realize the potential of their internal networks and comprehend fiber's importance as a strategic advantage in the increasingly competitive utility marketplace.[16]

While privately owned utilities are moving rapidly into these new business efforts, the publicly owned utilities have had a head start, partly because they have been allowed to provide these services for a longer time and have had to be more responsive to their customers, who, as taxpayers, are also their shareholders. Until very recently, regulation did in fact hamper the ability of investor-owned utilities to provide services in this market. This section discusses the activities of a number of municipally and privately owned utilities.

Privately Owned Utilities

CSW Communications in Laredo, Texas, established an energy management program, using advanced communications networks that saved its customers 7 to 10 percent on monthly electric bills.[17] CSW is a subsidiary of Central and Southwest Holding Company, which is a registered holding company with retail electric utility subsidiaries and the first to receive ETC status from the FCC under the 1996 Telecommunications Act. Under the Laredo program, the price of energy varies, depending on the time it is used. Customers use the rate information to help determine their usage patterns and save money. Price variations are noticed via computers, electronic sensors in the home, fiber-optic cable, and coaxial cables. The cost of connecting each home in this project was approximately $2,500. CSW is trying to reduce the cost to $1,000 per home.[18] CSW projects that the program might help its customers by postponing the need to build new generation and transmission lines. The program enables the utility to know the amount of electricity its customers use at each moment; to raise the price of electricity to discourage use and avoid brown-outs; and, with the customer's permission, remotely to disconnect appliances, such as air conditioners or water heaters, at peak times. Even with all these energy management services operating in Laredo, CSW still uses only 5 percent of the capacity of its broadband network, making uses that involve cable, telephony, and Internet access entirely possible.

CSW Communications will also build and operate an advanced communications and energy services network for the city of Austin, Texas. CSW's program will serve Austin's publicly owned Electric Utility Department and its 300,000 customers. The plan is for CSW to create a new network company, which will be a twenty-first century prototype for a "utility company" that will negotiate agreements with telephony, video, data, and information service providers. Together, the network of providers will offer demand-side management services, automated outages services, remote meter reading, and other services. The process has been delayed, however, by a Texas state law that was adopted just before the Act was passed. The state law has been challenged on the grounds that it hampers true competition and is inconsistent with the federal law. The FCC has been petitioned to review the Texas law for consistency with the Act.

In September 1996, the United States Department of Energy gave CSW a grant to develop an advanced energy management service, using personal computers and the Internet. CSW will conduct this project in Laredo, Texas, in conjunction with Los Alamos National Laboratory. The grant will allow CSW to expand its present services in Laredo to create an Internet service provider (ISP) operation and to test new, Internet-based energy management services.[19] The goal of the grant is to create a new model for energy efficiency and management services, which are part of the National Information Infrastructure and may help keep smaller metropolitan areas competitive.[20]

As of early October 1996, the FCC had granted ETC status to seven utility companies.[21] Even prior to receiving ETC approval for its new subsidiaries, the Southern Company was providing Internet, cable, remote monitored security, and energy management on a trial basis to an apartment complex in Chatelaine, Georgia. It was also operating an interactive on-line cable network in Duluth, Georgia, which provided television and energy management services. In conjunction with AT&T, the Southern Company is marketing its Enerlink information services for large customers and experimenting with other home energy management systems that may be used with its broadband network.[22]

A more recent and comprehensive example of a utility that is attempting to link its electric service to advanced communications services is the joint venture between Boston Edison and Residential Communications Network Inc. (RCN),[23] a subsidiary of WorldCom. Jointly, they will provide one-stop shopping for telecommunications and electric services for 650,000 customers in and around metropolitan Boston. They will invest $300 million in the joint venture and propose to provide local and long-distance telephone services, high-speed Internet services, cable television, and, eventually, energy management and property monitoring services to customers in the region. RCN has the controlling interest of 51 percent and will actually provide the communications services. Boston Edison is providing the infrastructure, using its 200-mile fiber-optic network.

TeCom, the telecommunications subsidiary of TECO Energy, Inc. (Tampa Electric Company), in Tampa, Florida, is developing and expanding a personal computer-based, interactive, home energy management project. TeCom manufactures and markets InterLane Interactive Home Manager, which offers energy management services, home automation, automatic meter reading, and remote connect and disconnect. It also integrates home security and advanced entertainment, such as digital satellite TV. The service is innovative and progressive in that it is technology-neutral. The open architecture of InterLane allows connections via telephone, cellular PCS, cable, fiber-optic, or satellite. InterLane can provide fast Internet access via any of these media. By partnering with a wireless communications provider as well as using its own fiber-optic network, TECO will have two-way communications with its customers.

Citizens Utilities in Arizona was honored with an award from the magazine, *Beyond Computing*, in 1996 for its efforts to align its broader business goals and strategies with its information technology operations.[24] Citizens Utilities provides communications services as well as gas and electric service. It is the fifteenth largest telecommunications provider in the United States. It proposes to offer Internet access to its customers in northwestern Arizona through an agreement with GETnet International Inc. Citizens Utilities will offer, over the Internet, local telephone dial-up, water, power, gas, and waste disposal services.[25]

In 1996, Utilicorp reached an agreement with Adaptive Networks, Inc., a leading developer of power line communications technologies, to develop advanced communications technologies, which will enable an AC power line to support a communications network, and to introduce these technologies on a global basis. Utilicorp is an electric and gas company with operations in the United States, Canada, England, New Zealand, Australia, and Jamaica. The U.S. division intends to provide its energy applications to all classes of customers wherever competition is allowed. The Adaptive Networks technology, a semiconductor chip that can be installed in computing devices and other machines, makes it possible to develop computer software, so as to be able centrally to monitor systems as various as air conditioners, telemetering, and vending machines.[26]

Publicly Owned Utilities

As stated earlier, publicly owned utilities have had a head start in providing advanced communications services to their customers. The following examples explain the genesis of these infrastructures, their links to core utility services, and their capacity to provide the last mile for other communications-based services.[27]

In 1994, the Public Utilities Department in Anaheim, California, decided to install a fiber-optic network to link the utility's facilities. The Department has a fifty-mile fiber network that it uses for utility, mobile data, and intersite communications. It has a SCADA system that controls grid transmission and other operations. The goal of the Anaheim Public Utilities Department is to provide a "universal telecommunications system" for the businesses and residences in the city of Anaheim, which would include demand-side management and energy-efficiency programs, time-of-use meters, automatic meter reading, data transfer, and telecommunications services.

In 1993, the Electric Light Department in Braintree, Massachusetts, began to build a fiber-optic network to improve internal communications. The department has subsequently used this network to link the city hall, high school, and fire department to the department's email and phone systems. Future plans include linking homes in the area to the network. These communications services, which are part of a bundled package of customer services, enable the utility to retain customers and give it a competitive advantage. The broadband services that Braintree envisions providing include automatic meter reading, geographical information systems (GIS) that map infrastructure electronically, cable television, Internet access, billing and load management, and electronic shopping for a local elderly housing complex.

The Public Service Department in Burbank, California, has had a fiber-optic network linking its major offices since 1987, and is looking at ways to provide load management programs and other broadband services, including cable video, data, and voice services. The department sees this network as an economic development tool that will link all city facilities and provide businesses with access to broadband information networks. In light of its location, the department has targeted businesses in the entertainment industry as potential customers and provides entertainment services, such as virtual reality, interactive viewing, and movies-on-demand. The Public Service Department's effort is viewed as a revenue-generating undertaking and a means of encouraging economic growth in the region.

In 1994, after extensive deliberations and validation by the voters, Cedar Falls Utilities in Cedar Falls, Iowa, decided to install a fifty-mile fiber-optic network. The network, which utilizes Cedar Falls Utilities poles, is designed to deliver broadband services to individual homes. It will also improve utility distribution and monitor usage via distribution automation and meter reading. It will be called the "Metro Area Network" and will offer Internet, electronic mail, video conferencing, high-speed data, video, and voice services. Its video services will indirectly compete with those offered by TCI.

The Electric Plant Board in Glasgow, Kentucky, receives all its electricity from the city of Glasgow, which purchases it from the Tennessee Valley Authority (TVA). In 1985, in order to reduce the cost of electricity, the Electric Plant Board instituted a load management program, which has since evolved into an extensive broadband network that includes video services, telephony, interactive video, and data networking. The system also provides economic development benefits to the community by offering video competition and disseminating information through its computer network links. It provides customers with cable service by direct connection to their TVs, with data through broadband interface cards in computers or file servers, and with a voice interface unit that provides a dial tone. The system costs $2.8 million to operate annually, which, on a per capita basis, costs $200 per person (population of 14,000). The savings from load management-related benefits alone are estimated to be $175,000 per year, or $12.50 per person. These figures, however, do not take into account the many externalities, such as improvements made to traffic signals, savings in video programming (Glasgow's video rates are among the lowest in the country), increased transparency in government through the broadcast of government meetings, educational networks linking the schools, and access to databases shared by schools, libraries, and even local real estate agencies. Future broadband services include home shopping, customized cable packages, and bank-at-home services.

The Water & Light Department in Newnan, Georgia, benefited from the city of Newnan's installation of a fiber-optic communications network. The city installed the fiber to improve the SCADA system, which helps monitor and control water stations, water towers and power distribution stations. Using the fiber network, the city installed an Ethernet connection to some of the city's businesses and schools and a T-1 connection for Internet services to city services, businesses and schools. Potential new uses of the network, such as video services, automatic meter reading and load management, and voice transmission, are being explored.

Fifty-three U.S. municipalities provide electric services. Among the eighteen that have internal communications infrastructure, all but one also have an external application for infrastructure. Projects are also being developed in places where incumbent carriers are not meeting the public need for Internet and other services. In Lincoln, Oregon, for example, the public school system has been linked to the Central Lincoln Public Utility Department's fiber network to provide schools with distance-learning capabilities and Internet access.

What Stands in the Way?

Despite the activities of many pioneering utilities, as a rule, utilities have not been quick to see the natural connections between communications services, their traditional business of selling electricity, and their new business of providing energy-related and other services and customer value. Some would argue that the utility industry is too entrenched in a monopolistic mind-set to succeed in such a competitive marketplace. These critics point to the mistakes that occurred when, in the past, utilities diversified into the real estate business and other nonrelated enterprises. They also point out that some attempts by utilities to enter communications markets have already ended in failure.

If the utility industry is to adapt, however, to a more competitive market for its traditional services, then the culture of utilities must also change. They must learn to make decisions more rapidly, to foster innovation internally, and to recognize the need for alliances and joint ventures with other companies that may help them adjust to competition. In the twenty-first century, using communications services to serve retail customers directly may become a part of the core functions of electric utilities and certainly will, I predict, for the most successful utilities.

The regulatory environment must support the evolution of the utility industry. The use of broadband and other communications-based customer services in the utility industry is part of that evolution. The Act has done a great deal to facilitate the transformation of the utility industry, but both regulators and utility executives may limit the role that utilities play in providing new communications-based services to customers, if they fail to see the natural link between the communications and utilities industries and the services that they provide.

A clear example of the kind of roadblock that must be removed is the Texas law that prohibits municipal utilities from providing telecommunications services.[28] ICG, along with other parties, filed a petition with the FCC to have the law preempted because the law frustrated ICG's attempts to lease space on the fiber-optic system operated by San Antonio's City Public Service.[29] The FCC issued a decision in the fall of 1997, which declined to preempt the Texas statute's prohibition of telecommunications services by municipalities.[30] This ruling was made on the ground that Texas municipalities were not separate entities from the state and that preemption would inappropriately insert the federal government between the state of Texas and its political subdivision. Since ICG withdrew its petition in the summer of 1997, the FCC did not decide whether the Act could bar the state of Texas from prohibiting the provision of telecommunications services by a municipally owned utility. Although the Los Angeles Department of Water & Power agreed to lease 105 miles of fiber network to ICG under a fifteen-year agreement, which strengthened ICG's position as a competitive carrier in southern California, the Texas law prohibited similar positioning in that state.

Most of the roadblocks are less obvious. They often arise from either regulatory or utility failure to see the linkages between providing quality utility service, on the one hand, and broadband and Internet services, on the other. Alternatively, regulators may fail to separate the need to address legitimate public interest concerns from the question of allowing utilities to participate fully in the communications market. For instance, in 1996, the Georgia Public Service Commission reversed a decision that would have prohibited a subsidiary of the Marietta Board of Light and Water from providing data transmission services to businesses in Cook County, Georgia.[31] According to Commissioner Bobby Baker, the Georgia Public Service Commission denied the municipal utility permission partly to "make certain a government entity cannot undercut competition by offering at or below costs services financed through tax dollars."[32] When the utility appealed the decision and explained that it needed to provide the services to compete in its market, the commission reversed itself.[33] Georgia law allows competition among retail electric companies for customers with loads above 900 kilowatts.[34]

As utilities face competition in the wholesale and retail generation markets, the question arises as to the manner in which utilities will recover the costs of assets that, as a result of competition, are no longer used. For example, if a utility loses a portion of its demand to a competitive service provider, how does the utility recoup the cost of the plant that is no longer used, due to competition? Such costs are called "stranded investments." What better way for a utility to respond to the threat of stranded investments than by providing customers with a value-added service, such as data transport, and thereby possibly retaining the customer and avoiding stranded costs? Despite all the emphasis that utilities and regulators place on cost recovery of stranded assets and investments, few utility executives or regulators have really focused on the potential of communications-related, value-added services to mitigate against the creation of stranded assets and investments.

A significant issue for utility executives as they consider entering these new markets is the perception of their entry by state and federal regulators. State regulators often do not fully appreciate the degree to which their reaction to regulatory issues affects the utilities under their regulatory authority. Regulators often think that utility executives should have enough independence from regulatory concerns to act as they believe necessary to benefit ratepayers and shareholders, regardless of the attitude of the regulators. Regulators are convinced that, if the statements of a utility executive are correct, she will be persuasive in the administrative proceedings. This is a fallacy. It is like a judge expecting all complainants in a civil trial to prove their cases, even though the judge may be scowling from the bench and complaining about the costs of attorneys and the need for the suit. Some complainants may choose to settle their cases, even when they are meritorious, rather than risk the judge's wrath or having to pay the opponents' legal fees. A few too many scowls from state regulators, even if those scowls are based on lack of information, may deter many utility companies from participating fully in the communications market.

Electric utility executives are particularly sensitive to the inclinations of their state commissioners because the electric industry is currently being restructured. The decisions that regulators make about industry investments in electric plants, the restructuring of the industry, and other matters will dictate the disposition of millions and, in some cases, billions of dollars of regulated assets. Utility executives refrain from being assertive about communications services, in order to protect the recovery of stranded costs, which they view as more important.

Meanwhile, regulators do have legitimate concerns about the entry of utility companies into the communications market that can and should be addressed without either purposefully or inadvertently discouraging utilities from entering the market. These concerns include:

• creating an environment for competition across and between industries;

• removing barriers to entry;

• eliminating unfair competitive advantages (e.g., cross subsidies, bottlenecks); and

• creating fair interconnection agreements.

State regulators will decide whether communications, electric, gas or water utility companies will be allowed to provide the same services in new ways and new services on existing infrastructures. Communications companies will not build generation plants and utility companies will not build switches. Rather, electric, gas, and water companies will become "virtual" communications companies and communications companies will become "virtual" electric, gas, or water companies. An example of a virtual telephone company operated by a utility might be as follows. A customer would buy from an electric utility company local exchange service bundled together with electric service. The utility would provide that service to the customer, even though the utility itself did not own or operate a communications switch. The utility, instead, is in a joint venture with a competitive local exchange carrier, in which that utility would provide the competitive local exchange carrier access to its fiber-based transmission network and the competitive local exchange carrier would provide local exchange service under the utility company's brand name. From the telecommunications customer's perspective, one company would provide all these services. From the electric customer's perspective, the communications-related costs for providing electric service would be reduced by spreading the underlying infrastructure costs over a larger base of customers. Both the telecommunications and electric customer would likely benefit. Customers in more rural parts of the country might only have access to broadband services through these type of virtual telephone companies, since the incentives for network investment might not otherwise exist. Redundant investments in new infrastructure would be avoided, the costs for communications companies to enter new marketplaces would be reduced, the costs of stranded investment would be mitigated, and there would be a broadband network that is truly ubiquitous and affordable.

Utilities' use of the communications infrastructure might also be a critical element in the restructuring of the electric utility industry. Utilities initially began to use communications technologies to explore the uses of broadband technologies and the Internet, in order to reach out to their customers and to provide effective energy-efficiency programs. The restructuring of the electric industry will force even greater use of tools, such as the Internet. For example, utilities have already developed an extensive Internet-based interface as part of compliance with the requirements of FERC orders 888 and 889, which address open access and stranded cost issues, require utilities to establish electronic systems to share information about available transmission capacity, and establish standards of conduct. If properly harnessed, utilities' entrance to the communications market might actually ensure ubiquity and high-quality service in both electric and telecommunications markets.

Any remaining restrictions under the Public Utility Holding Company Act must be clearly explained so that utilities will understand any limitations on their participation in the communications market. These limitations must not prohibit the development of virtual utility and communications companies, since such virtual companies are likely to be the best bet for ensuring truly ubiquitous, transparent, affordable access to the Internet and broadband service.

Another area in which legislators and regulators are critically important is in defining the roles of public and private utilities in providing these services. Municipal utilities should be encouraged to compete in the communications market. Competition may give rise to unusual arrangements. For instance, in Texas, CSW Communications, a subsidiary of Central and Southwest Holding Company that owns privately owned electric distribution companies, advocated that the FCC should preempt a state law that limits participation by the city of Austin in the communications market. The potential benefits to municipal utilities of their tax-exempt status or any other unfair competitive advantages have been debated in the electric utility restructuring forums and are beginning to surface as an issue in the telecommunications market.

The degree of success in eliminating biases stemming from tax advantages that municipal and other public utilities may enjoy, without prohibiting the use of publicly funded communications infrastructures for private uses, will determine whether the vision of ubiquitous and affordable communications services will be achieved. For example, in Iowa there is much debate over whether a fiber-optic network funded through state bonds should be allowed to connect with private hospitals and schools. A controversy in Georgia over the Fibernet project chiefly revolved around tax-related questions, rather than the benefit to business customers from using Internet services provided by utilities. This question affects institutions as large as the TVA and as small as the Marietta Board of Light and Water.

Of course, there are many transition issues that must be addressed before utilities may provide residences with broadband services. Regulators must balance the equities between incumbent carriers and new entrants, between entities that have bottleneck facilities and those that do not, and between municipal utilities and those owned by private investors. None of these transition issues, however, should detract from the goal of providing universally available access to advanced communications networks.

On the industry side, executives must find the right match for each utility. Not every utility will be interested in or able to provide end-to-end telecommunications services. In the near term, most utilities will remain facilitators of the new competitive telecommunications market by providing dark fiber, reliable and safe access to conduits and poles, and ancillary services, such as billing and collections. But, many utilities will find it beneficial for their core ratepayers and their shareholders to become providers of telecommunications services. These companies must participate more in the regulatory forums that will shape the communications market.

Utilities should become a critical component in achieving the vision of a populace that makes everyday decisions related to family, health care, education, government, business and recreation by using the most efficient tools and the most up-to-date information.

We are on our way to realizing this vision. An environment for competition across and among industries is being created, barriers to entry are being removed, unfair competitive advantages are being eliminated, and open access is growing. All these developments permit utilities to take their place with all the other new entrants in the exciting market for Internet and other broadband services.

Notes

1. Bernice K. McIntyre, "Entering the Telecommunications Common Carrier Market: Factors Every Utility Should Know," *UTC: The Telecommunications Association Report* (June 1996), p. 5.

2. Herbert Cavanaugh, "Information Superhighways Are Under Construction at Many Electric Utilities," *Electrical World* (February 1994) p. 5.

3. "Utilities in Telecom: A New Source of Power," Telecom Publishing Group report, Vol. 2, pp. 28–29.

4. FCC Fiber Deployment Update (1994), p. 10.

5. H.R. 3790, 104th Congress, 2nd Session, July 11, 1996.

6. Speech at the National Association of Regulatory Utility Commissioners' Winter Meetings, Washington DC, March 4, 1998.

7. *PUR Utility Weekly Letter,* No. 3275 (October 4, 1996), p. 1.

8. Transcript of interview with Tom May, Chairman of the Board, CEO, and President of Boston Edison, September 30, 1996, WBZ-AM Radio, Boston News.

9. Enron 1996 Annual Report.

10. Energy On-line, September 18, 1996, <http://www.energyonline.com>.

11. Ibid.

12. Telecommunications Act of 1996, Section 103(a).

13. Bernice K. McIntyre, "Entering the Telecommunications Common Carrier Market: Factors Every Utility Should Know," p. 12.

14. Telecommunications Act of 1996, Section 253(a).

15. *Energy Law Journal* 16, No. 1 (1995), pp. 121–125.

16. Bill Bassett, "Sole Provider," *Electronic House* (August 1996), p. 34.

17. CSW website, October 8, 1996.

18. *Austin American Statesman,* June 18, 1995.

19. CSW News Release, September 9, 1996.

20. Ibid.

21. The FCC has approved 15 companies as ETCs: CSW Communications, Entergy Technology Company, Entergy Technology Holding Company, NU/Model Communications, Southern Information Holding Company, Southern Telecom Holding Company, Southern Information 1, Southern Information 2, Southern Telecom 1, Southern Telecom 2, Allegheny Communications Connect, AEP Communications, Columbia Network Services, 280 Security Holdings, and NEES Communications.

22. EEI data, May 1996.

23. WorldCom is in the process of purchasing MFS, according to Dataquest.

24. Citizens Utilities press release, September 30, 1996.

25. *UTC's Business Wire*, October 8, 1996.

26. Utilicorp News Release, July 2, 1996.

27. *Utilities Telecommunications Guidebook: A Management Guide to Business Opportunities and Telecommunications Technologies for US Municipal Utilities*, Appendix B: Case Studies, prepared under a grant from the American Public Power Association's DEED program, 1996.

28. Public Utility Regulatory Act of 1995, as enacted by S.B. 319 Acts of the 74th Texas Legislature, Regular Session, 1995.

29. *Washington Telecom Week*, October 4, 1996, p. 19.

30. FCC 97-50, October 1, 1997.

31. *UTC Business Wire*, October 8, 1996.

32. Georgia Public Service Commission, "Media Advisory," July 2, 1996.

33. *UTC Business Wire,* October 8, 1996.

34. Georgia Territorial Electric Service Act, Georgia Code, Title 46, Chapter 3, Section 8.

The Emerging Municipal Information Infrastructure: The Austin Experience

Lon Berquist and August E. Grant

The city of Austin, Texas, is one of many local municipalities that have taken initiatives to develop an advanced telecommunications infrastructure for the benefit of their citizens, businesses, and institutions. These cities have been prompted by a number of factors, including: the prospect of local telecommunications competition; the concerns about the integrity of city-controlled rights-of-way as many competing telecommunications firms build their own exclusive telecommunications networks; the belief that an advanced telecommunications infrastructure contributes to local economic development in an increasingly competitive and techno-logical economy; the emergence of power utilities as telecommunications providers with energy information services; and the gradual maturing of digital telecommunications technologies.

This chapter addresses the role that may be played by municipal governments in promoting the construction of advanced telecom-munications networks. Following an exploration of technological and regulatory factors that underlie the entry of municipalities as players in the provision of the last hundred feet, the experience of the city of Austin is detailed. The chapter then concludes with a discussion of specific factors that should be considered by munici-palities as they consider their role in the provision of advanced telecommunications networks for their citizenry.

Local governments have a keen interest in the expected compe-tition among telecommunications providers because the bulk of the technical infrastructure for both cable systems and telephone networks are situated geographically and operationally within the domain of municipalities. It is the city streets and poles that provide the real estate where telecommunications companies place their wires and related hardware, including the last 100 feet, to reach homes. If, as anticipated, competition leads to the entrance of new providers and technological upgrades by existing telecommunications providers, it is the cities that will bear the brunt of ongoing street digging and related construction. Furthermore, for many cities, promotion of advanced telecommunications infrastructure is part of a broad strategic investment, which is meant to revitalize or sustain urban environments and to offer advanced services that may not be offered by incumbent telecommunications providers.[1]

The convergence of telecommunications technology and the increasing authority of municipalities to determine telecommunications policy offer local governments a new opportunity to assert their regulatory power. One of the most important implications of the entry by local governments in the United States into the process of implementing advanced telecommunications infrastructures is that a "bottom-up" conception of infrastructure development may be more appropriate than a "top-down" approach.[2] This perspective suggests that, instead of conceptualizing the U.S. telecommunications infrastructure as an "Information Highway," the focus should be on the "Information Main Street."

The Technological and Regulatory Context

While national policy has only slowly begun to establish a framework for the development of a national information highway, a number of municipalities quietly established their own information thoroughfares in the late 1980s using existing telecommunications infrastructure. These early municipal systems are called community computer networks, civic networks,[3] public information utilities,[4] or community on-line systems.[5] They are increasing in number, with networks operating or being proposed in over 100 communities throughout the United States.[6]

The growth of local community networks has been an important step in the evolution of the Information Main Street. At the same time, local telephone and cable infrastructures have technical limitations that prevent the implementation of many of the technological innovations touted by the federal government and by industry. These advances include education and distance learning, video-on-demand, high definition television, interactive entertainment, interactive program guides and navigators, civic networking, personal communications services, telecommuting, business services, research support, information services, Internet access, and telemedicine.[7] Cable television's traditional lack of switching capabilities inhibits the industry's implementation of advanced telecommunications services. Telephone technology's bandwidth deficit limits the role of local exchange carriers (LECs) in providing innovative services. In order to understand the manner in which cities may become players in this increasingly competitive marketplace, it is necessary to examine the technologies themselves more closely.

Telephone Technology

Cable television and telephone companies differ significantly in their technological architectures and their past regulatory schemes. Cable television has a broadband, passive transmission system, while the telephone infrastructure has a narrowband, switched architecture. The telephone industry has historically been regulated as a common carrier, while cable systems, though recently rate regulated, are free from the burdensome controls placed on telephone systems. Deregulation will allow direct competition between telephone companies and cable operators for both telephony and video programming. Gradually, telephone companies are expanding to wider bandwidths with the introduction of fiber optics and other advanced technologies. Cable operators are also looking to these technologies to help ease the transition to a broadband switched digital network.

There were only 283,000 miles of fiber optic cable in use for U.S. telephone service in 1983. That figure jumped from 1.24 million miles in 1986[8] to 5.6 million miles by 1991, and almost tripled to 16 million miles by 1994. For telephone companies, much of the transition from twisted-pair copper wire to fiber optic cable has been a natural part of the conversion from analog to digital signals, and from mechanical to computerized switching. Although the architecture for the telephone system has remained basically the same, the conversion from analog to digital has called for new digital standards and sophisticated digital switching equipment as well as fiber transmitters and receivers (transceivers) and fiber amplifiers (repeaters).

While fiber has been touted as the ideal medium for digital transmission of telephone conversations, fiber optics do not yet reach directly into homes. Digital transmission over twisted-pair wire, typically limited by lack of bandwidth, has been enhanced tremendously by innovative hardware and software advances over the past few years. The Integrated Services Digital Network (ISDN), which was meant to be the first step in the universal conversion of telephone service to digital technology,[9] has already been super-seded by new hardware and software that allows even greater efficiency in sending digital signals over various media, including fiber optics. For example, Bell Atlantic, in its bid to enter the video marketplace, has attempted trials in Virginia using Asymmetrical Digital Subscriber Line (ADSL) technology, which pushes the capacity of twisted-pair wire to a bandwidth of 1.54 Mbps, enough to send a channel of MPEG compressed video to subscribers.[10] Future refinements of ADSL should allow capacities of up to 6 Mbps for twisted-pair wire. Other experiments have pushed the capacity of copper wire to the Fiber Distributed Data Interface (FDDI) speed of 100 Mbps over limited distances.[11]

Cable Television

Compared to the telephone industry's early investment in fiber optics, the cable television industry's conversion from copper coaxial cable to fiber has been much more technically complicated and tentative, due to cable's passive architectural design. In order to take full advantage of fiber's greater bandwidth, cable has had to change from its tree-and-branch configuration to a fiber-to-the-feeder (FTTF) architecture.[12]

In a typical FTTF system, digital signals are sent from the "head end" of the cable system to transitional nodes, or hubs, where they are converted to standard radio frequency (RF) analog signals.

Each node sends the RF signal through a copper coaxial line to between 500 and 2,000 homes. The great advantage of this design, in addition to the greater bandwidth of the fiber, which allows for a potential of 500 channels, is that it eliminates the need for most of the signal-degrading amplifiers found in typical RF cable systems. While video signals must shoot through numerous amplifiers before they reach the home, a FTTF system needs only three or four amplifiers from the feeding node to the home.[13]

The design tested by cable systems—such as Time Warner's Full Service Network and Viacom's Castro Valley System—is a typical hybrid fiber-coaxial (HFC) system; digital video signals are sent to hubs via fiber and transmitted to homes using existing coaxial wire. ATM switching is used to handle the routing of the high-bandwidth digital video signals, along with video servers for storing video programs in digital form. In order to store the equivalent of a typical video rental store, future video servers would require a hard disk of 80,000 gigabytes, approximately the storage capacity of 100,000 PCs.[14] Digital television-top boxes receive the digital information that is transmitted through the fiber.

Electric Utilities

Electric utilities, a new and potentially strong competitor in telecommunications, are as ubiquitous as the telephone network. Utilities have access to rights-of-way that reach virtually every home, business, and institution in the United States. Utilities are primarily planning to implement telecommunications services for energy information services, such as demand-side management, customer-controlled load management, and remote meter reading.[15] These technologies allow cost savings for both the utility as well as the consumer through real-time pricing, automated billing, energy education, and energy sales.

Advocates of building the U.S. information infrastructure via utilities argue that many utilities already have an existing telecommunications component[16] and that, since little bandwidth is needed for energy management, substantial bandwidth is available for other telecommunications services.[17] In addition, utilities have substantial financial resources for building a communications infrastructure. In 1994, the ten largest registered electric holding companies held about $115 billion in assets, with profits of $3 billion.[18]

Regulated under New Deal legislation, the Public Utility Holding Company Act of 1934 (PUHCA), utilities have been restricted in their ability to use their ratepayer-based revenues for ventures unrelated to the provision of energy. With the passage of the Telecommunications Act of 1996, however, utilities have gained the opportunity to provide advanced telecommunications services to consumers.

In order to provide energy management services, many utilities initiated telecommunications services or developed partnerships with telecommunications service providers before the passage of the Telecommunications Act of 1996.[19] Increasingly, municipally owned utilities, such as the Glasgow Electric Plant Board of Glasgow, Kentucky, have developed plans for telecommunications networks, typically with fiber optics, to enhance the effectiveness of the utility and for city communications services. Holland, Michigan, Orangeburg, South Carolina, Austin, Texas, Denton, Texas, and Manassas, Virginia, are cities with municipal electric utilities that have developed or explored city-initiated communications networks.[20] Municipally owned utilities make up 14 percent of the U.S. customer base, while rural cooperatives make up 10 percent of electricity customers.[21] Time will tell if electric utilities can compete with cable television and telephone companies.

The Telecommunications Act of 1996

While technological enhancements are causing a convergence between cable systems and telephone networks, a policy convergence among federal, state, and local governments is also emerging. Before passage of the Telecommunications Act of 1996, the historic "natural monopoly" of the telephone network compelled regulation of interstate telephone service at the national level via the Federal Communications Commission (FCC) and regulation of intrastate service at the state level through state public utility commissions. Local governments' regulatory powers were limited to franchising cable television systems and managing city rights-of-way (ROW). The replacement of regulation by competition limits telecommunications regulations at all levels of government—federal, state, and local. Since, under the Telecommunications Act, cities retain control over their rights-of-way, the traditional two-tiered structure of federal and state regulation of telecommunications is rapidly evolving into a three-tiered regulatory structure, as municipalities firmly assert control over the physical rights-of-way used by the telecommunications industry. Although the federal government ultimately retains much of its authority over state and local jurisdiction, some see this devolution of communications policy as a natural result of deregulation.[22]

The goals of the Federal Telecommunications Act of 1996 mirror the aims of many municipalities—competition in the telecommunications marketplace. As the 1996 Act is implemented, however, its effect upon recent municipal infrastructure development efforts remains unclear. The bill preempts local regulation that might prohibit a business from providing telecommunications services but affirms the authority of local government to manage its public rights-of-way and to charge telecommunications companies fair and reasonable compensation for the use of those rights-of-way.[23] This provision, however, has already led to jurisdictional battles within some states, with the telecommunications industry attempting to bypass local authority over rights-of-way by dealing directly with state utility commissions.[24]

Under the Act, municipalities may continue to renew cable franchises, to collect franchise fees, to require public, educational, and governmental (PEG) access and institutional networks, and to include facility and equipment requirements as part of the franchising process.[25] Telephone companies that wish to enter the cable business must gain local franchises for the cable television portion of their service. Yet, municipalities are restricted from regulating the voice telecommunications services provided by a cable television system. The Act allows a telecommunications provider to become an FCC-certified open video system (OVS), without a local franchise, if the provider offers two-thirds of the system's capacity to unaffiliated programmers.

In addition to promoting competition, the 1996 Act charges the FCC with reforming the current financial subsidy system for universal service. A Federal-State Joint Board will review comments and make recommendations on replacement of the subsidy system with a method that does not impede competition. Their preliminary report calls for utilizing universal service funds to provide schools, libraries, and health care providers with substantial discounts for advanced telecommunications services.[26] As with national policy for universal availability of the telephone network, a goal of cities is for advanced telecommunications networks to reach every residence, business, and institution in the city. While the Act maintains universal service goals and promotes discounts for schools and libraries, it does little to promote access to advanced telecommunications services for residences.[27] Cities, which are excluded from the Joint Board, have a strong interest in providing advanced telecommunications services to all their residents. Recognizing that the Telecommunications Act did not anticipate jurisdictional conflicts between city, state, and federal regulation, the FCC created a State and Local Advisory Board to address issues of concern between states and cities.[28]

The City of Austin's Broadband Network

On April 11, 1996, the City Council of Austin, Texas, voted to negotiate a franchise agreement with Central & South West Communications (CSW) for CSW to build a hybrid fiber-coaxial (HFC) network to interconnect all homes, businesses, and institutions in the city. This vote was the final step in a two-year process of selecting a company to build a broadband network to provide telephone, cable television, digital video, and digital data services.

The process began with a "Request for Information" (RFI) issued by the city in June 1994. The RFI was designed to measure the feasibility of such a network and the level of interest among potential contractors, service providers, and citizens of Austin. The RFI set three goals for the network: that a network of optical fiber be constructed to serve the community; that multiple service providers have access to capacity; and that the fiber be installed, wherever feasible, through underground conduit.[29]

Thirty-four responses were received from prospective users, incumbent telecommunications providers, competitive access providers, telecommunications consultants, vendors offering specific products, and four prospective network providers, which submitted detailed proposals for construction, financing, and operation of the network. A committee consisting of private citizens, telecommunications experts, and city staff from the cable and regulatory services department and the municipal utility department met approximately every two weeks for three months to review and discuss the responses. The responses clearly indicated to the committee that the technology was feasible and that interest in the network was strong enough for the city to move forward to solicit specific proposals for operation of the network. The committee also realized that the city faced numerous decisions, including: whether the architecture of the network should be all fiber or hybrid fiber-coaxial; whether the city should own part or all of the network; whether and how the city should attempt to regulate the network; how the network would be financed; and whether changes in ordinances should take place to assist the construction and operation of the network.

Although most of the responses supported construction of the network, strong statements of opposition were received from three of the city's incumbent telecommunications providers: an executive with Southwestern Bell, the president of Austin Cablevision (owned by Time-Warner), and the publisher of the local daily newspaper, the *Austin American-Statesman*. In general, the incumbents argued strongly against any city ownership of or involvement in the proposed network, stressing the risks involved and the importance of competition in the private sector.

The committee's final report to the City Council, issued on October 25, 1994, recommended that the city issue a "Request for Strategic Partners for Telecommunications Infrastructure" (RFSP) for a public-private partnership to implement an advanced telecommunications network. Five specific areas were identified as key factors in the RFSP: the extent of the City's contribution to the partnership, timing, costs, financing, and management of the proposed network.

In response to the RFI Committee Report, the City Council authorized the committee to prepare the RFSP based upon the information contained in the RFI report. The RFSP was issued on March 7, 1995, and listed four policy objectives for the network:

1. *Open Platform:* Technical capability among network providers must be assured, as well as equal access to the network for all service providers. The network must be capable of being connected to other existing networks.

2. *Abundant Bandwidth:* To make the Open Platform work there must be available capacity beyond current demand insuring that access won't soon be denied for capacity reasons.

3. *Universal Availability:* Connections to the system are to be available to every residence, business, and institution in the city.

4. *Low Environmental Impact:* Construction and operation of the system must occur in a way that minimizes adverse impact on the environment and beauty of the community.[30]

The least ambiguous of these goals was that the network should be an open platform, with any potential service provider able to secure access to the network. The desire for "abundant bandwidth" was more problematic, as no one had a firm idea of exactly what the bandwidth requirements would be. The "universal availability" objective later proved to be one of the most important distinguishing factors among the proposals received.

The importance of the final objective, "low environmental impact," was the least apparent to those not familiar with the basic city services. While concern over environmental matters dominated a great deal of city debate, this item also represented a simple, operational idea: city streets should not be disturbed more than once for construction of an information network. In addition to creating traffic problems, "street cuts" may reduce the life of a stretch of pavement by up to 50 percent. If multiple networks were constructed, with each providing a separate service, the disruption and damage to the city streets might be very high.

The RFSP also stated the following five goals:

1. *Competition:* The City intends to stimulate competition by making capacity available to service and information providers. They may enter the market more easily by not having to bear the costs of building their own transport facility. A single open network allows more providers to offer more services at lower cost.

2. *Economic Development:* A first-class telecommunications infrastructure is a necessity in the emerging information economy. An

advanced public telecommunications facility will serve existing businesses and promote new ones throughout the Austin area.

3. *Asset Management:* By having a common public telecommunications facility, scarce rights-of-way can be used optimally, redundant infrastructure avoided, and disruptions and public costs due to construction minimized.

4. *Advanced Telecommunications:* The City seeks a public switched digital broadband network that supports two-way voice, data, video, and multimedia communications.

5. *Partnership:* The City prefers to form a strategic partnership with private enterprises. The City brings significant contributions to the enterprise and prefers a role with a greater degree of proprietorship than the traditional franchise arrangement. At the same time, the City prefers to limit additional public debt or risks to the taxpayers.[31]

One additional goal was stated elsewhere in the proposal. In all stages of the process, the city-owned utility had worked to spur the inclusion of utility applications in the network. In addition to remote meter reading, the utility was interested in using the network to implement "demand-side management" (DSM), a system allowing the utility to charge different electric rates at different times. Utilities are typically required to provide 110 percent of peak demand, leaving a great deal of capacity idle most of the day.[32] The key objective of DSM is to allow utility customers to shift usage from peak hours to nonpeak hours, thereby reducing the generating capacity needed from the city-owned generating plants.

The RFSP proposed an aggressive timetable, with proposals due by June 1, 1995, less than three months after release of the RFSP, and an expiration date for the responses of November 28, 1995. The expiration date indicated the date by which the City expected to select one or more proposals and commence—or complete— negotiations on the partnership. Ultimately, the due date for responses was extended and the negotiation process did not begin until April 1996.

Twelve firms responded in whole or in part to the RFSP.[33] Six of the proposals involved only a portion of the network or the equipment needed to construct the network. The other six contained specific, comprehensive proposals for construction, financing, and operation of a network. The least complete proposal consisted of a comparatively simple fiber backbone costing a few million dollars. The most comprehensive plan envisioned a complete fiber network that provided a fiber optic circuit to every home, business, and institution in the city at a proposed cost of over half a billion dollars.

In addition to significant differences in network architecture, the proposals also encompassed a range of plans for financing and operating the network. The financing proposals ranged from complete private financing and ownership of the network to complete city financing, using tax-free municipal bond packages. There was much less variety in the proposed management schemes, with most of the network providers proposing to manage both construction and operation of the network. The most optimistic proposals called for the proposing entity to sell equipment to itself at a significant markup, charge a management fee for operating the network, and receive a portion of the revenues from the network.

Following an initial review of all proposals, the committee (now renamed the RFSP Committee) invited each presenter to meet with the committee to answer specific questions. The committee had expected to complete its review and recommend one or more proposals for further consideration before the end of September 1995, but, by that time, the committee had only managed to narrow the list of proposals to four.[34] Over the next five months, the committee continued to review the proposals and to meet with the remaining contenders to determine which proposed system might best meet the city's goals.

Throughout the process, the committee deliberated the merits of different network architectures, business plans, financing arrangements, and timetables. But no aspect received as much attention as the degree to which the city would be involved in the day-to-day ownership and management of the network. On the one hand, city ownership or oversight of the network might ensure the goals of openness and universal access. On the other hand, it would require the city, with an already high bond debt, to take on a financial obligation almost equal to the city's biggest project to date, a new airport, with an estimated cost of just under half a billion dollars.

The turning point in the debate may have occurred in October 1995, when city voters were asked to approve $10 million in bonds to fund half of the construction costs of a new baseball stadium for a minor-league baseball team that wanted to relocate to Austin. Technically, the bonds were "certificates of obligation," which might be repaid only with revenues from the stadium, but voters overwhelmingly rejected the bonds in a vote that many termed a referendum on fiscal responsibility by the City Council.

Although many members of the committee seemed to prefer city ownership of the network, that level of involvement meant financing the network with tax-free municipal bonds. Committee deliberations kept returning to the consideration that voters were unlikely to approve bonds for a telecommunications network and that any such proposal would consign the proposed network to failure.

Another important factor was the passage by the Texas Legislature in 1995 of House Bill 2128, which prohibited municipal "direct or indirect" involvement in the provision of telecommunications services. The bill was shaky on Texas state constitutional grounds and the 1996 Federal Telecommunications Act seemed to preempt the legislation, but committee members knew that having the law declared invalid would require a legal battle. The committee was faced, therefore, with the question of whether the time and expense of mounting such a legal challenge would delay or derail the network.

In March, the committee met to make a final decision on which of the four short-listed providers would be recommended for further negotiation with the city. Each provider was rated in three areas: technical aspects, business plan, and viability and experience. No proposal received a perfect score. CSW Communications received the highest score.

Following the vote, the committee prepared a complete report of its activities, including the recommendation of CSW to build the network.[35] The recommendation was made public on March 26, 1996, at a meeting of the City Council's Telecommunications Subcommittee, which voted unanimously to recommend that the full council approve negotiations with CSW at its April 11 meeting.

Lessons from the Austin Experience

Although the Austin network will not be completed for some years, Austin's experience offers a number of lessons about the rapidly changing telecommunications environment, the choices that must be made in the process, and the resources that are available to any city that wishes to spur or to be involved in the construction of an advanced telecommunications network.

The telecommunications marketplace has been driven by technological change for the past two decades, as new technologies and applications have been developed for existing and potential networks. While any state-of-the-art technology may quickly become outdated as newer technologies are developed, a city that wishes to build a communications infrastructure must eventually decide on a particular technology, thus tying the future of a network to a technology that may be outdated before the full network is complete. There is always the option of deferring any decision indefinitely, however—see the Seattle experience, below. A related problem is that many of the most promising technologies are still on the drawing board, facing numerous unforeseen challenges in the implementation phase.

The other major force in the telecommunications marketplace is regulatory change. All levels of government, from city to state to federal, recognize the power and potential of emerging telecommunications technologies, with legislators and regulators working to protect their interests and, in most cases, to promote competition. Perhaps the best example of sweeping regulatory change is the 1996 Telecommunications Act, the first major revision of U.S. communications regulation since the Communications Act of 1934.

Cities pursuing an advanced telecommunications network must make at least three major decisions. The first is the degree of government ownership of the network. Public ownership may help to ensure realization of policy goals, such as openness and universal access, with concomitant risks related primarily to the debt that must be incurred to enable construction of the network. In addition, there are the perennial questions of whether governmental entities should be competing with private enterprise to provide telecommunications services and whether any governmental entity would be able to provide services as inexpensively as a private network.

The second decision is the network architecture. In 1999, the most proven technology is a hybrid fiber-coaxial system, which typically brings a fiber connection to a neighborhood node from which the signal is delivered to individual homes through coaxial cable.[36] The current "dream" technology is fiber optics, offering virtually unlimited capacity to all customers of the network. The cost of installing a fiber-to-the-home (or fiber-to-the-curb) system is, however, much higher than that of a hybrid fiber-coaxial system. There is no large-scale all-fiber community network yet in operation.

The third decision is the timing for construction of a network. It is impossible to choose a specific technology with the confidence that the technology will be the best one available at the end of the five or more years it will take to construct a network. The best strategy is to design a network that is able to be upgraded, with a business plan that allows for aggressive rebuilding and replacement at five and ten years, rather than the fifteen- to twenty-year life cycle of most telecommunications network equipment. Another solution is to build the network with upgrades in mind. For example, an HFC network may be constructed using a cable that contains both coaxial cable and fiber optics, with the fiber left "dark" (not activated) at the time the initial installation is completed. Since the installation cost (digging trenches, mounting cables on poles, etc.) is significantly more expensive than the cost of the cable itself, this plan may result in dramatic savings over the lifetime of the network as well as an easier upgrade to an all-fiber network.

The final issue is the range of available municipal resources. The following list identifies some of resources that a city may be able to commit to a network:

• *Utility poles:* Any city that owns its own utility will also own the utility poles that must be used for wiring a community. Furthermore, the city controls access to streets, under which most networks will need to run conduit or cables.

- *Government telecommunications needs:* Often, a city government may be one of the largest customers of telephone service in an area. Commitment of the city's business to the network will ensure a minimal level of business.

- *Existing fiber optic system:* Many cities have existing fiber optic networks constructed for internal use that may be made part of the backbone of a new network, reducing the upfront costs of building the network.

- *Municipal utility:* Demand-side management is one of the utility's key tools for reducing the need to construct expensive generating facilities. Although a telecommunications network is one of the most expensive means of implementing DSM, the fact that the network may easily be used to provide a variety of other services, including telephone, cable television, digital video, and Internet access, makes the network a good investment.

- *Ordinances and the permit process:* A city may make it easy or difficult for a firm to construct a network through its power to regulate construction and use of right-of-way. Use of this resource to inhibit construction of a network is not likely to be fruitful, but a city may use this resource as an enabling tool, making the process of obtaining permits or getting access to right-of-way easier for itself or for a provider that seeks to help a city achieve municipal goals related to competition, openness, environmental impact, or universal service.

Additional Examples of Municipal Information Infrastructure Development

Seattle, Washington

Seattle was the first city formally to request proposals from firms to build a comprehensive broadband telecommunications system. In January 1994, the city issued a request for information (RFI) seeking investors and developers interested in building in Seattle.[37] In October 1994, Seattle received 17 proposals in response to an RFP to build a privately financed telecommunications network.

Doubts about the financial viability of the proposed networks and concerns about the state of technology, particularly the availability and performance of digital customer premises equipment and ATM switching equipment, caused the city to abandon the RFP deliberations. When, however, Viacom sold its Seattle cable franchise to TCI in 1995, the city was able to achieve, in its negotiations with TCI, a major part of its stated goal of residential high-speed Internet access.

Anaheim, California

The city of Anaheim, with a municipally run electric utility and its own internal telephone system, received 18 proposals in June 1995 to develop a public-private universal telecommunications system (UTS) connecting Anaheim's businesses, schools, residents, and government buildings, utilizing 50 miles of the Public Utility Department's (PUD) existing fiber optic cable.

On January 9, 1996, the City Council authorized Anaheim's Public Utility Department to negotiate an agreement with SpectraNet International for the UTS. Construction of the system will be completed in two phases. The first phase, expected to take less than two years and cost $50–60 million, will connect commercial, industrial, and government buildings with fiber optic cable. The second phase, over five years, will extend the telecommunications system to residential areas. The telecommunications system will be privately financed by SpectraNet, with the city receiving a one time payment of $6 million and annual revenues of $1 million or 5 percent or gross revenues, whichever is greater, for its rights-of-way and existing fiber optic infrastructure.[38]

San Diego, California

San Diego issued an RFP through the San Diego Data Processing Corporation (SDDPC), a nonprofit consortium serving the city and regional agencies via the San Diego Network (SanNet). The SDDPC received eight proposals in January 1996 to build a "community-wide information infrastructure."[39]

San Diego allowed the respondents to develop either a private virtual network (PVN), which would enhance the telephony and data communications capabilities of the existing SanNet, or to build a more expansive regional telecommunications network (RTN), which would establish a regional, open, switched, digital broadband network. The city expected that the final project would be a private-public partnership with the city as an equity partner. During the city's deliberations, however, the Telecommunications Act of 1996 was passed, and the city reconsidered the entire RFP process. The process was abandoned, as in Seattle, with the hope that competition among private sector telecommunications firms, touted by sponsors of the Act, would lead to the goals expressed in the original RFP.

Other Cities' Experiences

Many cities, particularly those that own their own utilities, have developed or are considering developing advanced telecommunications systems in direct competition with their local telephone company or cable system. Cedar Falls, Iowa, has built a hybrid fiber-coaxial system that provides video, voice, and data services to residents, competing with the local TCI cable system. In California, Santa Clara, San Jose, and Palo Alto are considering utilizing fiber optic networks, built primarily for their municipally run utilities, for residential telecommunications services. In late 1996, the largest city in the United States, Los Angeles, announced a request for information to build a public-private telecommunications infrastructure.

Conclusion

It is important for the federal government, state utility commissions, and the telecommunications industry to recognize the roles that local governments play as regulators and potential partners in building the last hundred feet of an advanced broadband telecommunications infrastructure. The increasing number of city telecommunications initiatives suggests that U.S. information infrastructure, despite being coordinated and promoted at the national level, will be developed locally and regionally through the emerging infrastructure development efforts of municipalities.

Notes

1. Mitchell L. Moss, "Telecommunications and the Economic Development of Cities," in William H. Dutton, Jay G. Blumler, and Kenneth L. Kraemer, eds., *Wired Cities: Shaping the Future of Communications* (Boston: G.K. Hall, 1987).

2. Harmeet S. Sawhney, "Circumventing the Centre: The Realities of Creating a Telecommunications Infrastructure in the USA," *Telecommunications Policy*, Vol. 17, No. 7 (September/October 1993), pp. 504–516.

3. Richard Civille, "Building Community Information Infrastructure," *New Telecom Quarterly*, Vol. 2, No. 2 (1994), pp. 20–27.

4. K. Kendall Guthrie and William H. Dutton, "The Politics of Citizen Access Technology: The Development of Public Information Utilities in Four Cities," *Policy Studies Journal*, Vol. 20, No. 4 (1992), pp. 574–597.

5. Kathleen L. Maciuszko, "A Quiet Revolution: Community Online Systems," *Online*, Vol. 14, No. 6 (1990), pp. 24–32.

6. Douglas Schuler, "Community Networks: Building a New Participatory Medium," *Communications of the ACM*, Vol. 37, No. 1 (1994), pp. 39–51.

7. Cable Television Laboratories, "The Cable Connection: The Role of Cable Television in the National Information Infrastructure," white paper, 1995, <http://cablelabs.com>.

8. C. David Chaffee, *The Rewiring of America: The Fiber Optics Revolution* (Orlando, FL: Academic Press, 1988).

9. Loy A. Singleton, *Global Impact: The New Telecommunication Technologies* (New York: Ballinger, 1989).

10. Andy Reinhardt, "Building the Data Highway," *Byte*, Vol. 19, No. 3 (March 1994), pp. 46–74.

11. Patricia Schnaidt, "Twisted Pair FDDI," *LAN Magazine* (September 1992), pp. 19–20.

12. Nancy Jesuale, "Telco, Cable Cooperation Could Payoff," *TV Technology*, Vol. 11, No. 2 (1993), pp. 1, 8.

13. Reinhardt, "Building the Data Highway."

14. Frank Beacham, "Hype, Hope, and Reality," *Video*, Vol. 18, No. 5 (August 1994), pp. 36–39, 68.

15. Electric Power Research Institute, "Business Opportunities and Risks for Electric Utilities in the National Information Infrastructure," October 1994, TR-104539, Palo Alto, CA.

16. Michael R. Niggli and Walter W. Nixon, "Why Electric Utilities Should Build the Information Superhighway," *Telecommunications* (March 1995), pp. 68–74.

17. Steven R. Rivkin, "Positioning the Electric Utility to Build the Information Infrastructure," *New Telecom Quarterly*, Vol. 3, No. 2 (1995), pp. 30–34.

18. David Lapp, "Power Play," *Multinational Monitor*, May 1995, p. 11.

19. See the chapter by Bernice K. McIntyre for a detailed discussion of the telecommunications efforts of private and public utilities.

20. Clinton A. Vince, J. Cathy Fogel, and Paul E. Nordstrom, "Fiber Optics, Electric Utilities and the Information Superhighway—The Community's Role," *The Electricity Journal* (February 1994), pp. 34–45.

21. Rivkin, "Positioning the Electric Utility to Build the Information Infrastructure."

22. Robert M. Entman, *The Communications Devolution: Federal, State, and Local Relations in Telecommunications Competition and Regulation* (Washington D.C.: The Aspen Institute, 1996).

23. League of Cities, "The Telecommunications Act of 1996: What it Means to Local Governments," 1996.

24. Joe Estrella and Linda Haugsted, "Rights-of-Way: Cities or States?" *Multichannel News*, May 13, 1996, p. 6.

25. League of Cities, "The Telecommunications Act of 1996."

26. Federal Communications Commission, "Federal-State Joint Board on Universal Service: Report and Order: Universal Service Order," 1997, CS Docket No. 96-45.

27. Miles Fidelman, "The New Universal Service Rules: Less than Meets the Eye," *Civic.com*, Vol. 1, No. 3 (1997), pp. 30–33.

28. "FCC to Create Local Advisory Committee on Rights-of-Way," *Warren's Cable Monitor*, Vol. 4, No. 51 (December 23, 1996), p. 1.

29. City of Austin, "Request for Information: Telecommunications Infrastructure," 1994.

30. City of Austin, "Request for Strategic Partners for Telecommunications Infrastructure," 1995. p. 7.

31. Ibid, p. 8.

32. Rivkin, "Positioning the Electric Utility to Build the Information Infrastructure."

33. Proposals were submitted in response to Austin's RFSP by American Interactive (St. Petersburg, FL), CellNet Data Systems (San Carlos, CA), Central & South West Communications (Dallas, TX), Digital Equipment Corporation (Maynard, MA), Fincher, Inc. (Austin, TX), FNT Fibernet International Services Group (Tempe, AZ), Honeywell DMC Services, Inc. (Chelsea, MA), Industrial Construction Services, Inc. (Westminister, CO), InfoStructure (Menlo Park, CA), KCI Long Distance (Syracuse, NY), MCI Metro (Richardson, TX), and SpectraNet International (San Diego, CA).

34. In fact, the committee narrowed the list of proposals for further consideration to six, but two of the proposers removed themselves from consideration.

35. City of Austin, "Staff Recommendations for a City-Wide Open Broadband Network," 1996.

36. Robert Stanzione, "The Info Highway: Who's Going to be First?" *Communications, Engineering & Design*, September 1995, pp. 44–46.

37. City of Seattle, "Request for Proposals for an Information Highway," 1994.

38. City of Anaheim, "Universal Telecommunications System Partnership: Report to the City Manager and City Council from the Public Utilities General Manager," October 25, 1995.

39. City of San Diego, "Request for Proposals to Provide Telecommunications Infrastructure," 1995.

Contributors

Lon Berquist <berquist@uts.cc.utexas.edu> is a Ph.D. candidate studying Communication Technology and Policy at the University of Texas at Austin, where he is a Research Assistant for the Telecommunications and Information Policy Institute. He has worked for the IC² Institute at the University of Texas, the City of Austin's Office of Telecommunications and Regulatory Affairs, Stanford University's Networking and Communications Systems, and Viacom Cable.

David A. Beyer <dave@rooftop.com> is President and Founder of Rooftop Communications Corp., which develops sophisticated but easy-to-use wireless Internet software and systems. Prior to founding Rooftop in 1995, he worked for more than a decade on the research, development, and implementation of wireless and wired networks, including five years in a leadership role in the U.S. Advanced Research Projects Agency's packet radio program.

John Carey <JTCarey@aol.com> is Director of Greystone Communications, a telecommunications research and planning firm. He is also an affiliated research fellow at the Columbia Institute for Tele-Information at Columbia University.

David C. Carver <dcc@mit.edu> is Associate Director of the Research Program on Communications Policy at the Massachusetts Institute of Technology. He co-directs the Project on Local Access Communications. His research topics include multimedia storage and communications, electronic commerce and intellectual property, and convergence and interoperability of high resolution systems and broadband networking. He participates in government and industry forums, promoting the definition, design, and deployment of broadband communications and interactive services.

David Gabel <davidgabel@aol.com> is Associate Professor of Economics at Queens College of the City University of New York. His research has focused on both the evolution of telecommunications during the first competitive era of telephony (1894–1913) and current developments in telephony. His recent work focuses on the pricing of interconnection in network industries, the cost structure of the telecommunications industry, and retail pricing of network services under conditions of rivalry.

J. J. Garcia-Luna-Aceves <jj@cse.ucsc.edu> is Professor of Computer Engineering at the University of California, Santa Cruz. He is the co-author of *Multimedia Communications: Protocols and Applications* (1998). Prior to joining UCSC in 1993, he was a Center Director at SRI International in Menlo Park, California.

Branko J. Gerovac <bjg@mit.edu> directs the High Resolution Progressive Scan Camera Project at Massachusetts Institute of Technology. Prior to this he was Associate Director of MIT's Research Program on Communications Policy, where he co-directed the Project on Local Access Communications. His research interests include: the combination of technology and business modeling in the digital television, cable, and video server industries; investigating technologies to enable cost-effective high-bandwidth local access communications; and exploring open mechanisms for copyright and billing of new media. Previously, Gerovac was a visiting scientist at MIT's Media Laboratory as well as a consulting engineer in the corporate research group at Digital Equipment Corporation (DEC) and a strategic advisor to DEC's Executive Committee. At DEC and in cross-industry forums, Gerovac developed and managed R&D projects in the areas of workstation software and hardware.

August E. Grant <agrant@2wire.com> is Director of Research and Entertainment Services for 2Wire, Inc., in Milpitas, California, where he specializes in research on new media technologies and consumer behavior. A former broadcaster, his primary interest is mass communication technology. He was Associate Professor and founding Director of the Center for Mass Communication Research in the College of Journalism and Mass Communications at the University of South Carolina. Prior to that, he headed the Communication Technology and Policy sequence in the Department of Radio-Television-Film at the University of Texas at Austin. He is the editor of the *Communication Technology Update* (now in its sixth edition), a review of the latest developments in over three dozen technologies in electronic mass media, telephony, consumer electronics, computers, and satellites.

David R. Hughes <dave@oldcolo.com> is Principal Investigator for the National Science Foundation's Wireless Field Tests project. He is a partner in Old Colorado City Communications, an Internet and custom communications development company. He has been developing, operating, installing, and supporting online systems since 1979, concentrating on grassroots-up development of community and educational networking. He has consulted for the U.S. Congress Office of Technology Assessment and is currently advising the FCC on use of wireless for education. In 1993 Hughes was awarded the Telecommunications Pioneer Award by the Electronic Frontier Foundation for his work in grass roots electronic democracy.

Deborah Hurley <deborah_hurley@harvard.edu> is Director of the Harvard Information Infrastructure Project <http://www.ksg.harvard.edu/iip>. From 1988 to 1996 she was an official of the Organization for Economic Cooperation and Development (OECD), with responsibility for legal, economic, social, and technological issues related to information and communications technologies, biotechnology, environmental and energy technologies, technology policy, and other advanced technology fields. In the field of information and communications technologies, she initiated and carried out work on computer services, database services, value-added network services, cryptography technologies and policies, security of information systems, intellectual property protection, and privacy and data protection. She was responsible for the drafting, negotiation, and adoption by OECD member countries of the 1992 OECD *Guidelines for Security of Information Systems.* She is a member of the Advisory Committee to the U.S. State Department on International Communications and Information Policy and cochair of its Working Group on Security, Privacy and Export Controls. She is also a member of the Advisory Board of the Electronic Privacy Information Center (EPIC).

Andrea L. Johnson <alj@cwsl.edu> is Professor of Law at California Western School of Law and Director of its Center for Telecommunications. The original version of this 1997 article was published in the *Nova Law Review* (Spring 1997). Her related article on the "Legal and Regulatory Issues Confronting Cities in Developing Interconnected Fiber Optic Networks: San Diego Model" was published in the *Rutgers Computer and Technology Law Journal* (1994).

James Keller <keller@lexeme.com> is Vice President and a Founder of Lexeme, Inc., and a Fellow at the Berkman Center for Internet and Society at Harvard Law School. Prior to these activities he was Associate Director of the Harvard Information Infrastructure Project until June 1998. He has authored and edited numerous books and articles, including *Coordinating the Internet* (with Brian Kahin, MIT Press, 1998) and *Investing in Innovation* (with Lewis Branscomb, MIT Press, 1998).

Bernice K. McIntyre <bkm@bkmcintyre.com> is Founder and Principal of B. K. McIntyre & Associates, Inc., a national consulting firm headquartered in Washington, DC, that advises telecommunications and electric utility industry clients on strategic regulatory and management issues. She has served as Commissioner (1983–1990) and Chairman (1987–1991) of the Massachusetts Department of Public Utilities. Prior to opening her own company, she worked for five years in the utility and telecommunications industry management consultancy of Arthur D. Little, Inc.

Milton Mueller <mueller@syr.edu> is Associate Professor at the Syracuse University School of Information Studies, where he directs the Graduate Program in Telecommunications and Network Management. He is the author of *Universal Service: Interconnection, Competition and Monopoly in the Making of the American Telephone System* (MIT Press, 1997), *China in the Information Age* (CSIS, 1996), and *Telephone Companies in Paradise: A Case Study of State Deregulation* (Transaction, 1993). His current research examines trade in telecommunications services, Internet governance and interconnection issues, and digital convergence.

Michael Propp <mpropp@adaptivenetworks.com> co-founded Adaptive Networks with his brother, David, and is President of the company. Dr. Propp is the co-inventor of the technology and holds key patents in power line communications technology as well as patents pending in both power line communications technology and power line communications applications. He is a U.S. representative to the IEC for Technical Committee 57, Working Group 09, Distribution Automation Using Distribution Line Carrier Systems.

Steven R. Rivkin <srrivkin@msn.com> is a telecommunications lawyer in Washington, DC, who advises electric utilities, telecommunications providers, and the U.S. Department of Energy concerning common opportunities in telecommunications and energy. Two of his recent monographs have achieved wide attention— "Short-Cut to the Information Superhighway: A Progressive Plan to Speed the Telecommunications Revolution," co-authored with Jeremy Rosner for the Progressive Policy Institute of the Democratic Leadership Council (1992), and "Positioning the Electric Utility to Build Information Infrastructure," for the U.S. Department of Energy (1995). Mr. Rivkin was a member of the White House staff during the Kennedy and Johnson administrations.

Mark D. Vestrich <marko@rooftop.com> is President of TeleScope Ltd., a company that grooms early-stage technology start-ups for success. He was formerly with Intel Corp. for fifteen years, where his responsibilities included developing new businesses in supercomputers, digital video, and wireless communications and managing strategic planning for all semiconductor products.

Bryan Vu <bryan-vu@trilogy.com> served as a policy analyst at the Federal Communications Commission in Washington, DC, during the second half of 1996. In addition to his work on satellite issues, he participated in projects dealing with international telecommunications development and the implementation of the Telecommunications Act of 1996. He has also worked as a software test engineer at Microsoft Corporation in Redmond, Washington, and at Flintridge Consulting in Pasadena, California. He is currently working as a consultant at Trilogy Software in Austin, Texas.

Index